Although this book was written for those who have lost a child, it is even more significant for those who have not. It will encourage every parent to realize and appreciate what precious gifts our children are. Trials and tribulations will come and go, but your children and the memory of them, live forever.
— Beth Beck
Coffee and Comfort facilitator
A group for mothers on Marco Island who have lost children

From an incomprehensible loss comes this story of inner torment, personal struggle, and strength of a father who has lost his little girl. A child's death strikes everyone as atrocious and most of us retreat from even thinking it possible. This extraordinary book lets the reader into the very personal secret internal processing with the twists and turns of emotion that can only come from a loving parent suffering from this type of loss. Although enormously sorrowful, this book creates hope and displays recovery through a true cherishing of joyful memories and honoring of life.
— Steven E. Smith, Psy.D., BCIAC, CCBT
Licensed Clinical Psychologist

The most powerful thing a memoir like this does for us is to teach us how to help. We can feel so helpless, so unable, so empty of anything worth giving. Roger, through your memories of Kendall, you let us know that we really might be able to offer some help and support even though we feel so powerless.

Chapter 14 was the core of the book for me: What word does any human language have for one whose child has died? How about "friend." That is so true and foundational and humbling. And it gives me my assignment: be a friend. I can handle that. I can give the gift of presence. It takes the intimidating fear of how to "fix it" away and tells me just to be there alongside. Accompany. Don't worry about what to call anyone, or what to say. It's an important reminder to us all.

Sleepless Nights also reminded me to keep in mind those in my own life whom I could contact on a difficult anniversary. I have started a list and want to follow through, letting them know they aren't the only ones who are thinking about their child. I thank you for that, too, Roger.

God bless you and all who love Kendall . . .

— Chaplain Mark Bartel
Manager, Spiritual Care
Arnold Palmer Medical Center

Sleepless Nights

The First Ten Years

Roger K. Moll, Jr.

Llarrie + Shirley
Peace through Remembering
[signature]

KELLER PUBLISHING
MARCO ISLAND, FLORIDA

Designed and composed in Bernhard Modern
at Hobblebush Books, Brookline, NH, USA

Printed in China by Sunquest (Shanghai) Inc.

ISBN: 978-1-934002-04-9

Published by

Keller Publishing
590 FIELDSTONE DR.
MARCO ISLAND, FL 34145

800-631-1952
www.KellerPublishing.com

To Kendall. . .
the greatest gift I ever received.

Thank you for teaching me then,
and continuing to teach me now.

Illustrations

Foreword

Remembering and Marching On

June 21 will forever be a day in my life to remember two very dear people. My grandmother died that day in 1985. Even though I was not ready for that phone call, I knew that my grandmother had lived a full life. In 1996, it was the death of my daughter's best friend, Kendall Jeanne Moll, daughter of Roger and Nanette Moll. I was not ready to receive that phone call. June 21, 1996 was the start of a journey for my dear friends that continues to this very day.

The death of a child has to be the most difficult experience of grief one can walk through. How do you continue the journey of life? How do you make it through birthdays and holidays with only the memory of your child? Life is always moving forward and yet how does a parent move with it when they have the constant reminder of a life that was much too short? You are about to encounter answers to these and other questions in the pages of this book.

Roger Moll, father of Kendall, allows us a personal glimpse into the world he has lived since first finding out about Kendall's death. His words are piercing and heart wrenching. They are cathartic and transforming. Roger's words have brought much needed relief to other parents who have joined the silent association he and his wife Nanette find themselves members of as they both share their pain and recovery with countless parents whose own children have died.

Read these words and you will pray for parents throughout the world who live every day contemplating days that will never happen. Read these words and continue your own personal journey of living life each and every day.

Rev. Durwood O. Foshee, III
Pastor, Trinity United Methodist Church
Palm Beach Gardens, FL

Preface

When memories are the only thing you have to hold onto, you never want to let them go. I started to write what you are about to read a few weeks after my only child, Kendall, died. I am not a very talkative person and find it much easier to verbalize my thoughts on paper.

These writings are a way for me to keep my memories from slipping away. It also offers me a way to free my mind of these thoughts.

My hope for you as you read them is that you find that you are not the only one going through the torture of losing a child. I know that I am not experiencing the same things that you are right now, but we do have many things in common.

These writings keep the memories of Kendall always there. I hope that as you read these that they will bring back memories of your child. It has been ten years since I have been able to touch Kendall physically, but with this book I know we are together.

I still cry everyday, some sad tears and some happy tears, but they are tears of being a Daddy. If you feel like crying, it is okay and I will cry with you.

May your journey to peace be a short one.

Kendall's Daddy

Sleepless Nights
The First Ten Years

1

Never discourage anyone…
who continually makes progress,
no matter how slow.

PLATO

I was thrown into a catastrophic event that changed my world. That event was the death of my daughter. It took me ten years to even start *wanting to attempt* to live again. This decision was slow in coming; yet, it wasn't quite as difficult as the next one. *"How do I begin to live again?"* I was slow in saying "Good-bye" because I just never wanted to say it.

The start of the process was deciding *how* to say, "Good-bye," and then finally actually saying it. For ten years your bedroom stayed the same. Finally being convinced that YOU would want me to be happy and live life, I wanted, yes wanted, to re-decorate your bedroom. After gathering ideas on what to do to the room, the hard thing was to clean the room out and pack your things.

Gathering boxes to put your things in led to the day that even though the room would always be yours, it wouldn't look like the room you'd lived in. Your toys, clothes, bed, and all the treasures you'd gathered were packed up. Some of these were to be saved as our treasures of you, some given to other family members so they could have treasures from you, and the rest was given as a gift from you to other families in need. The choosing of things for other family members made the transition a little easier. We were looking for things to give to family so they would forever have something of yours; the packing and cleaning came second.

Painting the walls, picking out the new floor, buying new furniture, and gathering new decorations all followed. Although redecorating is still not completely done, progress is being made, however slowly. The room still has your presence in it. There is a stripe of your purple paint colors on one wall and a piece of your Lion King Wallpaper border in the corner.

I continue to wish you were still here, and think of "Daddy things." The other day I was up in your tree outside our bedroom trimming some branches, when all of the sudden chills came over my body. I suddenly realized that I had forgotten to tell you that your room is being redecorated. It was as if you were away at college and you weren't told. I was trying to figure out how to tell you, when suddenly, I realized, I just had. I remembered that you weren't here on earth and I didn't need to tell you physically.

Kendall's Daddy

2

*If all difficulties were known
at the outset of a long journey,
most of us would never start out at all.*

DAN RATHER

The most significant journey that anyone can make is
that with a child. This journey for me started at 2:20
pm on February 27, 1987 in Mease Hospital in Dunedin,

Florida. Nan and I were presented with a 7-pound, 7-ounce, 20½-inch long baby girl. Her presence came only after a long period of labor and then finally a C-section. Our daughter was named after both Nan and me. My middle name, "Kendall" together with Nan's middle name, "Jeanne" became the given name for our little girl, Kendall Jeanne Moll.

It wasn't until the next day that we found out why Kendall couldn't be delivered naturally. She had a condition called Hydrocephalus (water on the brain). It was caused by aqueductal stenosis (the tube that drains the constant flow of brain fluid away from the brain was blocked). This condition caused her head to be enlarged, so it just wouldn't fit through the birth canal. With the exception of this condition, Kendall was a perfectly healthy baby. The hospital sent us home with instructions to call a pediatric neurosurgeon at Shands Hospital of the University of Florida in Gainesville. The next day we made the call to Dr. Parker Mickle, only to be told to get in the car and get that child to the hospital right away. Being new parents, this was the first time that we thought our baby was in danger.

At six days old on March 5, 1987, Kendall had a VP shunt implanted. This was a tube inserted to drain the fluid from her brain to her tummy. This tube ran from inside her brain, down the back of her head to the side of her neck, all just under the skin. From her neck it continued into her tummy, draining the excess fluid. The operation went very well with just the minor complication of Kendall having a little trouble coming out from the anesthesia. We were released from the hospital and sent home to return for follow-up visits every month. Our life was off and running now.

This is when the sleepless nights started. Not only from the normal care that a newborn requires, but also from the worry and concern of how our child would grow up. But with grace, Kendall grew and developed just as any child would despite the complicated start. On one of our check-ups with Dr. Mickle, he pointed out that Kendall was developing a lazy eye. It was suggested that we take her to a Pediatric Ophthalmologist. Dr. Bruce Hess diagnosed Kendall with "Strabismus" (lazy eye). Initially, we patched her good eye to strengthen the muscles of her lazy eye. Later, on December 29, 1987 Kendall had the first of three eye surgeries on the muscles of her lazy eye. The outcome of these surgeries provided Kendall with near perfect vision and no need for glasses.

Kendall was growing up into quite a child. She was a skinny, blonde-haired, hazel-eyed little girl who enjoyed life to its fullest despite the fact that she was self conscious of her "Badges of Courage" on her head and chest.

She looked so cute standing on the front porch of the house dressed in a cute polka dot dress carrying a lunchbox for her first day of Kindergarten at Tommie Barfield Elementary School on Marco Island, Florida. From this day forward she excelled in school, always wanting to learn, read harder books, and beat the boys across the monkey bars (which she could do if she wanted to).

Early in her second grade year, Kendall started to develop headaches, a frequent upset tummy and she was just not feeling good. Finally, it was traced to her shunt. It had become detached and was not draining properly. Back to Dr. Mickle and on September 24, 1994 she had an operation to repair her shunt. This would be her fifth operation in her short life so far.

Family was very important to Kendall. She always wanted to be together with her mom or me. When she could, she would travel to see her grandparents, aunts, uncles, and cousins whom she called her brothers and sisters (since she was an only child). For a time we lived with my parents, so she grew up with one set of grandparents very close by. Kendall and my mom developed a great bond; they both loved to shop and to do arts and crafts. Kendall wanted to do everything her cousins did, so she became quite involved in sports. She wanted to try everything, from horseback riding to cheerleading and on to baseball.

Kendall became quite involved at church also. She regularly attended with Nan and became an Acolyte. She felt comfortable there and understood.

You could never tell that Kendall had gone through so much thus far in her short life. She never let anything bother her and took everything in stride. She was a joy to be around.

Then on June 21, 1996 at 7:26am at 40 pounds and 4'4" long she left us on Marco Island, Florida to travel on a long difficult journey by ourselves.

Kendall's Daddy

3

Remember the day your daughter was born?

I do like it was yesterday!
Remember the joys and fun times you shared with your daughter?

I do like it was yesterday!

Remember when your daughter walked into the room with her first prom dress on?

I won't be able to!

Remember when your daughter graduated high school and college?

I won't be able to!

Remember the sparkle in your daughter's eyes as you walked her down the aisle of the church to be married?

I won't be able to!

Remember the first time you were called "Grandma" or "Grandpa"?

I won't be able to!

Remember the day your daughter died and all your dreams and hopes were no more?

I do like it was yesterday and will for the rest of my life!

Kendall's Daddy

4

The Day the Tunnel Got Dark

"*Roger, I did everything I could do.*"

Words that I never thought I would have to hear. These words brought life, hopes, wishes, dreams and especially joys to an end. Events that seemed would never arrive, never will. Things taken for granted are forever gone—never to take place again. Special events in the planning need not be completed.

Now different decisions have to be made. What do I do now? What is life going to be like? Is it going to be worth living?

What was important yesterday seems irrelevant today. What was irrelevant yesterday is of the utmost importance today. Family, friends, feelings, and making it through the day take precedence over all other things big and small. Work, money, and possessions; *Who cares?*

Losing the biggest, most important part of my life is a hard thing to comprehend. Worry, remembering, and experiencing a new life is all mixed together. This makes life very confusing. Many questions that arise will never be answered. That's the hardest thing. Did we ever do that together? I wish we were able to do that. We did that. I wish we were able to handle that differently. I hope it was okay that I handled or did that a certain way. Always thinking, *"Did I do my best? Did I put all my heart and soul into it?"*

The biggest and most difficult thing to accept is that all the wants, questions, and needs of my child are being taken care of and I have no control or input anymore. For this being such a beautiful thing, it is also a sad-depressing idea. It's another of those ideas that plague the mind. I wish I still had or could regain the privilege of being her parent again. But, of course, I realize that this is impossible.

Kendall's Daddy

5

It is very difficult to live among people you love and hold back from offering them advice.

AESOP

Welcome to the club; the worst club in the world. This is a club that you never want to be a part of, but are forced to join. This is the club that you automatically become members of when your child dies before you; something that is just un-natural. It's just not supposed to happen. It's a club that only members are able to really understand how you feel. People that aren't members don't know what to say to you. With all my heart I wish that you hadn't become a member. Children are wonderful, full of joy and happiness. It's just not right.

Hopefully, the thoughts that I am putting on paper for you will help you a little now, but I really doubt it. So my suggestion is to put this in a safe place and read it in about two or three months.

Your child is in Heaven, no doubt about it!!!! You know Heaven is a wonderful place; there is no better place in creation. It is a place where they will have no more sorrow, hurt or tears. Just a place where they can be themselves and not worry about anything; they are safe. You don't have to worry about them. They were carried to Heaven by Jesus and gently given to God who is taking care of them now and for eternity. They are in a place now where they will have an everlasting life. That's a very long time. Their life will never end now, not like yours will here on earth. You will be with them someday. It is going to seem like a very long time to you before you see them again, but that is using *your* vision of time. *To them*, right after their next nap you'll be with them. Their "time vision" goes on forever and ever. Their day, year and lifetime, if put into your "time vision" are milli-seconds. Maybe even smaller than that. So you can see, to *them* it is not going to be a very long time before you are reunited again. Best of all, this time it will be in Heaven for all of eternity! It is only *you* that for your lifetime here on earth, feel that it is a long time until that anticipated day.

There are some words in the English language that honestly ought not to be used ever again. These are SHOULD, WOULD, and COULD. Just take them out of your vocabulary and things will be a little easier. Not much, but at least a little. Don't become a "Monday Morning Quarterback." You can't change the past, no matter how much wishing you do. You *can* do things differently from now on and change the future though. You will never know if you'd have done something different if the outcome would have been any different. Don't let these three words shape your feelings and make matters worse. It is going to be hard to do this, but you have to try.

Another word that I am sure has come into your mind a few times is WHY. There have likely been two directions with this word, one is the *how* they died, and the other is *how come* they had to die. The how they died, I'm sure you will find out if you haven't already. That knowledge is very important in your grieving process that you are and will go through. The knowledge of why they had to die is the other part. Was it something you did or didn't do with your life? Does your child have another job to do? Or just, "Why the hell did they have to die?" You will never know the reason for their untimely death until you get to heaven. But really, does it matter? If you ever find this out here on earth, will it bring your child back to you? I'm sorry to say the answer is NO. So don't worry yourself with trying to figure out what the purpose of their death was. Someday when the time is right and you are together with your child in Heaven, you will find out the reason. So what is the hurry in trying to figure that out?

You know, life just sucks at times. There are going to be days that you just don't feel like getting out of bed and then there will be days when it is going to feel like you're trying to run up the down escalator. When this is happening you can't fight it. You just have to accept it and hope the day gets over quickly. Just get through the next minute and then the next minute, pretty soon the day will be over. As time goes on, things will get easier. Never really easy, you will just be able to handle them better. You'll gain a knowledge of how to keep yourself going and make it halfway up the down escalator before you are carried back to the bottom. You just have to keep fighting and pretty soon you will be getting further up the escalator. You will also find ways to cope with everyday life, when things seem they can't get any worse. For me, when things get this way, especially close to special dates and the stress of life builds, I tend to wander. I just get in my truck and drive. Nowhere special, I just go. You can ask my wife. I will walk up to her and tell her "I'll be back in awhile. I need to wander." I can't tell you where I go on these trips, they only last one or two hours and then I'm home. You will develop your own special way to cope with life from now on.

I guarantee your child will be sending you signs that all is okay. You too will start to do your own special things as a sign to them that you're starting to do okay too. For my family, the rainbow is a sign from my daughter Kendall that all is okay and that she is watching out for us. As you can see, I have a rainbow on my wrist as does my wife. Rainbows are pretty much on everything I own. Now let me tell you, I do get a lot of funny looks and sometimes even propositioned. But now a few more people know what the real reason is that I have a rainbow as a symbol. There are only a select few individuals that have a child as a guardian angel.

My paperwork is only done in the color purple ink. This is another symbol to Kendall that I always remember her, always will love her with all my heart and soul, and am counting the days until we are reunited again.

My wife and I have a few miles under our belt on the journey that you are just beginning. If you ever need anyone to talk with, cry with, or help with life in these trying times, please do not hesitate to call. It would be our extreme honor to help you through this.

Welcome to the worst club in the world.

Kendall's Daddy

6

We do not stop playing because we grow old.
We grow old because we stop playing.

ANONYMOUS

"Let me introduce myself, I am Kendall's dad."

That is probably the proudest thing I can ever say. In a short amount of time I learned so much from my daughter that continues with me today and has been the foundation of my life. In fact, she continues to teach me. Many people may see me and wonder, "What's up with this guy?" while I am looking for that teddy bear in the clouds, or puzzling why you can see the moon during the day sometimes, or even smiling on a gloomy, rainy day. You just have to remember that sometimes life is hard. Go back to the simplest things. Everything will work itself out, and then life will become bearable again. This, my friends, is what a child can teach you if you just listen to them.

Do you remember the first playground you played on? Mine was at Harbordale Elementary School in Ft. Lauderdale; specifically it was on the monkey bars. Our PE teacher was talking to us about being able to make it all the way across what seemed to be a mile of bars, but in actuality was maybe 10 feet. He told us the best way to get our bodies in shape to be able to complete this feat was to start water-skiing to build our upper body strength. So guess what? I asked my dad that night to go out and buy some water-skis. Well, after drinking half of the intercoastal waterway, I learned how to water-ski, and by the end of the school year had mastered those monkey bars too.

The time on the playground can teach our children many things and build their self-esteem; which in turn will enable them to conquer any obstacle they may face in their futures. Problems, challenges, fears, and self-doubt may be less of a problem because the play here can build the foundations needed to conquer life.

If you ever are having a hard day, just stop by the playground and listen. The laughing, yelling, screaming, and even crying, is medicine to the heart. It will help you realize that a smile on a child's face will do you good. So not only has the church built a beautiful playground for our children, but also built a get-well center for everyone. I guarantee that if you stop by here with a frown on your face you won't leave with it.

Now, please realize that I am not a religious person. But I am going to end this with a Bible verse and a challenge to everyone, young and old. The verse is Matthew 18-3. "And He said, I tell you the truth, unless you change and become more like little children, you will never enter the kingdom of heaven." Now the challenge is to EVERYONE, before leaving today you must use at least one piece of equipment on the new playground. I guarantee that you will leave with a smile on your face.

Oh, by the way, I smile on rainy days because I know I am going to see *a Rainbow*.

Kendall's Daddy

7

You never lose anything, not really. Things,
people, they go away. Sooner or later.
You can't hold them any more than you
can hold the moonlight. But if they've
touched you, if they're inside you,
THEN THEY ARE STILL YOURS!

MARIANNE KEANE
9/11 MEMORIAL

L osing a child is the worst thing in life that could ever
happen to a human being. It just plain SUCKS! You
think your life is over. For me things that hit hard are
that I will never see her laugh at me when I complain how
much money she just spent on that prom dress; the high
school and college graduations that won't be celebrated;
being able to walk her down the aisle of the church to be
wed; and never to be called Grandpa. I lost the events of
our life together, but she is still in me. Just ask my wife.
Kendall is very much inside me keeping me alive, young,
and attempting to enjoy life. Nan is always wondering,
"Where did that idea come from?" Sometimes she just

thinks I'm crazy. But let me tell you, that is just Kendall inside me.

My biggest wish in life would be to hold my daughter just one more time and tell her how much I love her. But just as the moonlight is untouchable, so is Kendall. But let me tell you, she is very much inside me. She is, and always will be my daughter.

You lose that ability to touch them, but I guarantee they're still touching you. They are constantly sending signs and signals to you that they are still around and watching you. Whether it is a rainbow or feather floating in the sky, their signs are all around.

Angels are wonderful things to have around. They keep you company, protect you, and for me answer many hard questions that pop up in everyday life. I am constantly asking Kendall questions on what I should do and I solicit her opinion. She always gives me things to think about and always starts her thoughts with "Well Daddy, . . . " and then just sort of rambles on. I talk to her everyday. Some days, I get the response of "Hey, I'm really busy up here having fun playing. Can we do this some other time?" I just have to think, well she is still inside me, and this is the exact same response she would have given me if she was here, so nothing has really changed.

Kendall's Daddy

8

Don't cry because it is over;
smile because it happened.

THEODOR SEUSS GEISEL

At first you don't ever think you will smile again. I sure didn't. Crying because *it is over* is all you do. Thinking about it being over and about never enjoying life again. Remembering all the past things that made you smile, just leads to the crying. The joys, accomplishments, happy times, and just goofy things that you did together flood through your mind. Even though they were great times, you can't smile about them now because the sadness of it being over is greater than the joy that these times once brought.

Remembering puts you in quite a predicament. You never want to forget the past, but the sadness of it *being over* makes you want to run from it. So at the start you try not to think about the past even though you never want to forget about it. Let me tell you, that is all you tell yourself. *"I never want to forget the smallest detail about the past."* Then, when you think about it you get sad and start the process all over again. So in the beginning, it's pretty hard to smile; all you really do in the beginning is the crying.

As life goes on, remembering the past becomes a little easier, *just a little*. The crying is still there and most likely always will be. However, the great sadness that once overcame you upon realizing there are no more memories to make is reduced with time. Not by much, but the pain is less. Maybe not "less," but at least easier to deal with.

As time moves on and these events get further into the past, you worry about forgetting them. So as things get easier to deal with in the moment, you start to try and remember things of the past. Suddenly you may feel fear as you remember what it was like initially with the cycle of remembering, then crying and becoming so sad. But now distance with the past is on your side and things are becoming slightly more comfortable with remembering the past. You may find you don't fear the sadness that once overcame you, because the joy of remembering is becoming greater and more desired. The sadness that comes is now more bearable.

Now, finally, you are able to smile when you cry.

Kendall's Daddy

9

I know God will not give me anything
I can't handle. I just wish that he
didn't trust me so much.

MOTHER TERESA

Just how much can you handle? You will never *really* know because you will never get there. Everyday life is simple. *Yeah right!* Think of all the things you do without thinking, the things that occur automatically. Your heart beats, you breathe, and you are able to walk.

But, when a major catastrophe happens in your life these everyday things continue to occur. You start to question yourself, life, and God. Wondering *how* to go on with your life is a major concern; possibly even *if* you want to go on. Somehow things build up and pile up on you and then they sort of level off for a bit. As this is happening, God is taking control, giving strong hints to your subconscious to take it easy and things will be okay. You can even start to think that you don't really want to breathe, but God made your body, so it does it without you even thinking about it.

It is okay to question God, but don't think that you are going to get any answers right away. They will come someday, maybe not in this lifetime, but you will find out why things happened the way they did. You may not like the reasons, but there's not much you can do about that. Acceptance is the only thing that can help. You know it is even okay to curse at God and tell him how you feel; it will help you relieve some pain.

Immediately after your catastrophe, take things slowly; minute by minute. Slowly go through life. It occurs all around you involuntarily, but you must remember to tell yourself to breathe. You need nice deep cleansing breaths. It helps clear your mind. Give yourself some easily attainable goals to grasp for. Accomplishing them will give you a sense of achievement.

Slowly, you will start to regain the ability to continue with life. It may take a while. It may even take a long while. You must realize that you will never regain life as it was before; it has changed drastically. As time goes on, God will relax His grasp on you and allow you to progress in your new life.

God takes over when you can't handle life or its circumstances. He will never push you over the edge. You may *feel* as though you are going over the edge, but then He holds onto you and protects you. You just have to trust Him as much as He trusts you. After awhile, you may wonder how you were able to get through all that you have been through. Well, you weren't alone.

Kendall's Daddy

10

Dreams surely are difficult, confusing, and not everything in them is brought to pass for mankind. For fleeting dreams have two gates: one is fashioned of horn and one of ivory. Those which pass through the one of sawn ivory are deceptive, bringing tidings which come to naught, but those which issue from the one of polished horn bring true results when a mortal sees them.

HOMER, THE ODYSSEY

I am told that dreams are messages from God. The message of the dream may be of face value or it may have to be processed. Dreams tell you things that you want to know, or things that will be changing or have changed.

My first dream after Kendall died is still my most remembered and vivid. It is of a young, blonde-haired girl standing in front of a corner cabinet bookshelf filled with books, videotapes, and tiny stuffed animals. The room is a little dark, since there was only a small window high on one wall, and the room had wood paneling on all of the walls. The girl is standing in front of the cabinet looking through the books while tossing a baseball up and down with her left hand.

In all my dreams of Kendall, I have never seen her face. But by the shape of her body, stance, and color and cut of her hair, I am sure it is she. The other thing I am quite sure of is that this room is the office/den/guest room downstairs in my sister's home in Cumberland, Maryland. Kendall loved going to my sister's home to visit her aunt and three cousins during summer vacations.

Since this dream was my first after Kendall's death, I believe that the message to me is that Kendall is okay. *Kendall is doing what she really loves to do*. Reading, watching videos, and playing with Beanie Babies (a collection that she was just starting and of which my sister has a very large collection). Plus, she is also at one of her favorite places.

Her cousin Adam was not with us at Kendall's memorial service. He did, however, send a baseball for Kendall to take with her forever. Baseball was something they had in common. Actually, Kendall played every sport that Adam played: soccer, basketball, and baseball. Baseball was a bone of contention between them. Adam loves it, and Kendall hated it saying it was too boring. She didn't mind telling him that. The baseball in my dream was the same baseball that Adam sent for Kendall to keep. To me this was just another sign that Kendall is doing okay and still has all the gifts that her family gave her.

So, Kendall is doing great, having fun, reading,

watching videos, playing sports, and doing little girl stuff.

But, where is Kendall really? She is just on an extended summer vacation.

Kendall's Daddy

11

REMEMBER ME

Remember Me . . . in a bible cracked
and faded by the years.
Remember Me . . . in a sanctuary
filled with silent prayer.
And age to age and heart to heart,
bound by grace and peace.
Child of wonder, child of God, I've
remembered you, remember Me.
Remember Me . . . when the color
of a sunset fills the sky.
Remember Me . . . when you pray and
tears of joy fall from your eyes.
Remember Me . . . when the children
leave the Sunday Mass with smiles.
Remember Me . . . when they're old enough to
teach, old enough to preach, old enough to leave.

MARK SCHULTZ

In a bible faded by the years... Somehow our children that have gone to heaven seem to have such an unbelievable grasp and understanding of God. Each time I hear a story about a child's understanding of what comes hard to me, I am just in awe of them. It's said that they're Old Souls, those who already have a deep understanding before their time. They accept and go in peace.

Remember me in silent prayer. I think not. Anything but silent. The two just can't go together. They enjoyed life. I just always hoped that Kendall could somewhat curb her zest for life during church services. It was me in the silent prayer; praying that she wouldn't burn the church down or light the priest's hair on fire carrying the acolyte torch down the aisle.

Child of Wonder, Child of God. Always exploring, always spirited. Have you ever tried to answer a child's question of, "Why can you see the moon during the day?" There seems to be an infinite number of "Why?" questions that they come up with while enjoying God's vast and awesome universe. They enjoy creation in a spectacular way; finding creatures in the clouds, running through a field of daisies barefoot, or just enjoying nature.

I do always remember you when the sunsets or a rainbow fills the sky, or a feather floats peacefully by. Signs abound, you just have to recognize them. They are for you, no one else. That's why no one else can see them. Every time you get one, just remember your child, say "Hey," and thank them.

Talk to your child everyday. I do. Ask for help from them. They will send answers and guide you along through your day. Tears of sadness will turn to tears of joy. Maybe not today, maybe tomorrow, but sooner or later. Then when your tears come, it will be not from the sadness of missing your child, but from the joys and fun times you are remembering.

Old enough to teach, old enough to preach, and old enough to leave. Our children begin teaching us the day they are born. We learn patience, love, and humility just to name a few. After Kendall left on her extended summer vacation in Heaven, she has continued to teach me. I now have learned that you have to enjoy life and not take it so seriously. Change is okay. It has to be, because life sure has changed without her. Your child will continue to teach you. Whether it's from college, after their marriage, or ultimately from Heaven, there are still things you can learn from them and their lives. I do know one thing that I have learned from Kendall and adopted into my life, and my family can attest to it: Growing old is required, but growing up is voluntary.

One puzzling thought I am continuing to work through is: *Am I like Kendall or is Kendall like me?* Parents don't teach their children, they guide them and let them go. But I continue to think that Kendall is still guiding me, and I have a long way to go, so she better not let go of me just quite yet. She continues to force me to keep growing both mentally and physically. I have accepted the mental part, but keep fighting the physical, middle age spread.

Kendall, I wish you didn't have to go so soon. Please keep that guiding light close to me. I promise you that I·will keep trying to enjoy life and never grow up.

So I offer what Kendall has taught me to you. Please keep growing but never grow up!

Kendall's Daddy

12

*Give us children's eyes, O Lord,
that we first may see the simple truth.*

REV. BO CHAPMAN

W hy does it often take a catastrophic event in one's life to make us see the simple truth?

Is there really any difference between birth and death?

As the celebration remembering the birth of Christ arrives, we are given the eyes of a child to see what gifts we have been given. Why are we unable to see these gifts without this ability? They are for us. All we have to do is just accept them, and still, we need the eyes of a child to lead us to them.

The death of my child, Kendall, has led me to the gifts also. Her birth, like any, was a miracle. She started with a fight and kept fighting throughout her short life here on earth. At an early age of six days, she began leading us to the simple truth, "Life is precious and a great gift to all. Take it and learn from it."

Throughout her life she battled many times, but always kept fighting. Never giving up, always going on, and accepting what she was dealt. A positive outlook was always around her. She showed us that life, no matter how grim-looking, is a great adventure and should never be taken for granted.

I am told Kendall had a grasp beyond her age of what the "Gifts from God" meant. She shared what she knew with everyone through her personality. She gave everyone her "eyes to see the simple truth."

She gave me the gift of yearning to grasp the same outlook for the gifts of God. Although I am not a religious man, I am a very spiritual man. Everyday I am in awe of the gifts of God. The earth, sun, moon, sky, freedom, the ability to choose, and I thank God for them and thank him for giving me the eyes of a child to see the simple truth.

Kendall's Daddy

13

Living one day at a time,
Enjoying one moment at a time,
Accepting hardship as a pathway to peace.

REINHOLD NEIBUHR

Does it really make sense to plan for the future? What about for tomorrow? For that matter, what about today?

It seems to me that planning for something that you can't control is a very difficult task. Does anyone really know what your future will bring? Are you planning for it?

What happens if everything that you have planned for disappears one day? What if you give up certain things or don't do things so that your future will be a certain way, then one day you learn that what you planned for won't happen. All those days invested are lost and can't be brought back.

The pathway to peace is a hard road. There are going to be many hazards in the way, hills to be climbed, and roadblocks that need to be conquered. Why not live one day at a time, one moment at a time? Those moments that turn into days once they are over can't be brought back. How sad if my only thought was that I wish I had enjoyed that moment more gloriously because I can't get it back to do all over again.

Remember the days that you delayed for the future?

Live each day to the best of your ability and make the most of every moment of the day; for it is these moments that are going to be the memories of tomorrow. Understand that even though you do this the roadway to peace is going to be very difficult. Forget trying to plan for the *what-ifs*; it is not worth the effort and pain to try and control them.

So why not just enjoy today and deal with the moments of today and do your very best with them? Then wait until tomorrow to see what it will bring, since your destiny is already planned.

Kendall's Daddy

14

*We call that person who has lost his father,
an orphan; and a widower that man
who has lost his wife. But that man who
has known the immense unhappiness
of losing a friend, by what name do we
call him? Here every language is silent
and holds its peace in impotence.*

JOSEPH ROUX

What do you call someone who has lost a friend? Ever think about that one before? That is like asking what you call a parent who has lost a child. Neither of these has ever been answered. Maybe because no one wants to deal with the issue; most don't want to face either of these unnatural occurrences.

Some are forced into either one or both these situations. One is bad enough, but both in one lifetime is unthinkable. It really hurts when you lose your best friend who turns out to be your child too. The person that you played with, learned with, and enjoyed life with. *What are you called now?*

Lonely, lost, unhappy, and grief-stricken all rolled into one body. There is no one word that says what to call that person. People don't know how to talk to this person even in normal everyday life situations, let alone trying to communicate with them during their time of grief.

The person that you once knew as a whole person, but since has lost part of their self, guess what? Don't call them anything different. Don't talk to them any different. They are still the same person.

My child/best friend is still with me and always will be, as will be your friends. Kendall is still teaching, for she has all the secrets. She is still playing, for she has the biggest playground of them all. And especially, more than ever, she is enjoying life; for she has a never-ending one now.

Really, you don't need to call us by any title. You don't even have to talk. The most precious gift that you may give is *presence*. Your presence in our lives.

If you really want to know what to call someone who has lost a friend, or a parent that has lost a child, here is your answer. Call them your FRIEND and just be with them as they go through their journey in search of peace.

Kendall's Daddy

15

If we don't change, we don't grow.
If we don't grow, we aren't really living.

GAIL SHEEHY

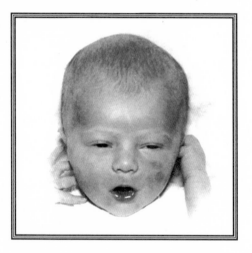

Your life changes the minute they are born and never stops changing. It is the most joyous change that you will ever experience—that moment your child is brought into this world. Growing up you always went the other way when responsibility came around. Now in one brief moment you face it head on and accept it with no questions. That child is depending on you to guide them through life's journeys.

Your life changes, your child changes, and your world changes. You are in a constant state of change and a constant state of growing. Living life is fun. Watching your child grow and experience the wonders of life is fun.

Then suddenly one day your life stops changing in this way. You want your life to continue the way it had been going. You were changing, growing with your child, and you were really living. But it can't be that way ever again. You truly want everything to stay the way it was. You may even try not to change anything in your world in an attempt to keep your life the way it was, so the happy memories never leave you. Nonetheless, you turn sad, for your changing force is no longer with you.

Staying this way isn't really living. The memories will never leave you, you will always remember the happy moments in your life, the changes that your child brought you, and the experiences that you went through together.

But after living and not changing for a time, you will soon learn that your child doesn't want you to remain stagnant in this way. They still want you to change, to grow, and to really live. Change doesn't have to be drastic, it doesn't have to occur overnight, and subtle changes are fine.

They still want you to go on living life to its fullest, even doing the goofy things that you did together. When you are living they are still with you, riding on your shoulder protecting you, guiding you and still experiencing life with you.

Kendall's Daddy

16

There is still no cure for the common birthday.

JOHN GLENN

I remember the first one. You came into this world after a long fight, only then to relax under a lamp with sunglasses on, and in the buff too—getting that all-over tan. You seemed to work on that tan like that all the time. From that day forward, we always looked forward to celebrating your birthday in some wild and crazy ways.

The next one was the first of many "Happy Meals." I picked out a cheeseburger for you, but as with most things you had your own idea and from that point forward it was "McNuggets." Every birthday that followed had its own special celebration.

You made everyone's birthday special. You wanted them to know that the day was *their* day and they were special to you. From the gifts you picked out, to the cards you made, everything had a special meaning to it. You were the cure for the common birthday.

I still look forward to February 27th in a special way. But now I wonder: If you were still here, what would we be doing? What would life be like? How would our life be different? Would you still have those chubby little knuckles?

This day is the happiest sad day of the year as we celebrate the day that you joined us on our life's journey. But you have gone ahead of us in your journey and are waiting for us to catch up. Still you are protecting us, going ahead making sure all is okay for us; sending signs—from making rainbows to growing white roses for your special people to enjoy and meditate with.

Women always seem to worry about getting older and seem to pick an age and remain that age forever. You will always be a nine-year-old, happy-go-lucky young lady that was beyond her age. Perhaps you knew the answers to life. You had already figured out everything that ladies try to understand well into their lives and just never seem to grasp.

Happy Birthday! Your birthdays surely didn't start out like a common one and from then on have never been common. They all had, and still have, the zest and wonderment for life that you share with your family and friends.

Kendall's Daddy

17

*In three words I can sum up everything
I've learned about life: It goes on.*

ROBERT FROST

It goes on. Yep, it does not matter how much you wish it did or didn't go on. Your child is born, begins to grow and you wish it could last forever just like this; spending your days enjoying your child as they grow in mind, spirit and body. To watch them as they first learn to roll over, then progress into crawling and finally watching those first wobbly steps.

As they experience the world, their mind and spirit expand in a phenomenal way. Their eyes are always wide-open taking in all of the wonders of the earth and its beauty; storing all they have seen and experienced for future needs. I also learned so much as I watched Kendall grow up, watching her experience life and become a young lady.

As you travel through life with your child, you both learn new things. You begin to enjoy life in a different way, and things that were important in the past don't hold the same value. You have a new outlook on life. Life is great!

Enjoying family and life become of prime importance. You change your being so these two things can happen. Then, for some, the unthinkable happens. Your child dies. This is something that seems to go against all of nature's laws.

Abruptly, your storybook life is in a shambles. You don't know which end is up. Everything that you have worked for, built, changed, and wanted for your family just disappeared. You don't want your life to go on. Your new life that was so wonderful isn't so wonderful anymore, and you don't like it.

But as time passes and you have time to reflect on your life, your child's life, and your family's life, you will realize that your child, although not *physically* with you, will always be with you. They would want you to continue life and live it as enjoyably as if they were physically with you. That one single thing is the hardest thing they can ever ask you to do. This will be a struggle, but knowing that *they* would like for you to do this, will make it a little bit easier, knowing that you can do it for them.

So, no matter what disaster may strike you and your family, life will change. But one thing is for certain . . .

LIFE GOES ON.

Kendall's Daddy

18

Read, every day, something no one else is reading. Think, every day, something no one else is thinking. Do, every day, something no one else would be silly enough to do. It is bad for the mind to be always part of unanimity.

CHRISTOPHER MORLEY

One of my favorite pictures of Kendall is when she was one and a half years old. She was relaxing on the couch in the living room reading a book. Well, I suppose she was pretending to read. From that point on whenever we left the house along with her toys and dolls there was always a book or two. As she grew older, she always had a book to read with her.

Kendall was born with a birth defect that was corrected when she was six days old, and from that point forward she put it behind her and took on life with a vengeance. She enjoyed her school years at Tommie Barfield Elementary School and life on Marco Island, being involved in as many things as she could possibly fit into each of her days.

While attending Tommie Barfield, she was very involved in the Reading Renaissance program. An avid reader, she was awarded the "World-Class Reader" certificate at the end of her third grade year. Kendall died just a short time after receiving this award.

The Association of Professional Firefighters of Marco Island has honored Kendall each year by giving a savings bond to a graduating fifth grade student who has displayed Kendall's zest for reading, thinking and learning, and general zeal for life.

Here is a list of the recipients to date:

1998 – Vanessa Warner
1999 – Chenoah Gutierrez
2000 – Mabelle Torres
2001 – Carolina Diaz
2002 – Chelsea Fletcher
2003 – Lior Frey
2004 – Megan Amos
2005 – Dylan Young
2006 – Mary Gibler

What a wonderful honor.   *Kendall's Daddy*

19

Don't limit a child to your own learning,
For he was born in another time.

RABBINICAL SAYING

For whatever reason, I never really had to worry about limiting Kendall to my learning. From the first day of school until her last, she took it on with a vengeance. She absorbed all that she could and wanted more. To her, learning was easy.

Kendall had the natural ability to structure herself, to maximize herself, to grasp anything that was placed in front of her. Don't get me wrong, there were things that she didn't like to do and it was a struggle to wade through them, but she pursued and completed the tasks at hand.

A major influence on Kendall was her three older cousins, Sam, Adam, and Kacie. She saw that they excelled in school and had time to enjoy life too. What she observed from them ranged from cheerleading and sports to science projects, and a vast array of extra-curricular activities. Because of this she wanted to do everything her cousins did.

She had plans; boy did she have plans. She was going to be a Sports Doctor in practice with Adam. That way, during baseball season Adam would be able to take the time off to play and the practice would have coverage. She knew that being a doctor would afford her the money to buy a big boat with a tall tower on it.

Not many people have the knowledge of how to raise their child from the very beginning. You might have read books or gathered ideas from other parents or your own parents. But mostly you do what you think is right at the time, and likely that is how you were raised or at least wanted to be treated.

I look back and thank Sam, Adam, and Kacie for the outstanding examples they set for Kendall. But, more importantly to their parents, for not limiting their children's learning to their own.

Kendall's Daddy

20

*The thing always happens that
you really believe in; and the belief
in a thing makes it happen.*

FRANK LLOYD WRIGHT

I remember the day that Kendall learned to ride a two-wheeled bike. She had been practicing on it with training wheels for a long time. It seemed it would be a long time and a lot more practice before she would be able to actually ride without the training wheels. She really didn't seem to have balance or control of the bike. Then one day she came to me and asked to take the training wheels off. I asked her if she thought she could ride the bike without them. She said she did and told me to just take them off. So the wheels came off and we headed for the street. Well, she fooled me! I was only able to run alongside her for a short distance, when she took off riding the bike like she had been doing it for years. *She believed.*

There is a tree in our back yard that was planted shortly after Kendall died. It is a memorial to her. I wanted to have a place for her to climb and be the monkey that she was. No matter where she was she would always find a tree to climb in *and up*. Heights didn't seem to scare or bother her. She wasn't satisfied until she was as high as she could be. To make it worse, when she got to the top she would yell out to you so you would come over to her. Your stomach would do flips seeing how high she was. She had no fear.

Throughout life you too will arrive at many obstacles that will need to be overcome. Learn from a child and remember what they will teach you: Believe in yourself. Have the self-confidence to know that you can do the unknown without the fear of failure. Treat failure as a learning experience; mistakes aren't a bad thing, but something to learn and grow from.

A child has no expectations. So nothing has ill consequences, only open futures.

Like Kendall, take off those training wheels and climb the highest tree around. Believe, and it will happen.

Kendall's Daddy

21

Did you ever know that you're my hero,
And everything I would like to be?
I can fly higher than an eagle,
'Cause you are the wind beneath my wings.

LARRY HENLEY AND JEFF SILBAR

I never got the chance to tell you so many things. I thought I had a lifetime. I didn't know our time together would be so short.

Kendall you are my Hero! From the day you were born you taught me never to give up, no matter how much crap was thrown at me. Everything can be conquered, no matter how gray the outlook is. I remember the first time I ever saw you. You were lying under a sunlamp in your birthday suit with some shades over your eyes working on your all-over tan. You'd just come through the most traumatic event of your life and you found time to kick back and relax.

You had a bright outlook and looked forward to each day. You were always looking for adventure, always looking for new experiences. But the utmost was never taking things for granted. Kendall, you showed me that life isn't perfect, but you can accept that, go on, and deal with it

50

the best way you can. Just smile and enjoy life no matter how difficult it is; knowing that tomorrow will be better.

Even the most ordinary events you made extraordinary. That's because you found unusual, funny, and even exciting things to do in everyday life. Always asking, trying to learn, you made me wonder about things just like you did. From the sea to the sky, that was ours to try and figure out. Those were the things that made you go, "hummmm."

You always made others feel special. Making others laugh and smile was your strong point. Doing this seemed so easy to you. You had a knack for doing it without even thinking about it. People could be having the darkest day, you could walk into the room and the sun would come out for them.

Kendall, you are my hero and everything I would like to be! You taught me more than I could ever teach you. I thank you for that and will forever cherish our memories. I love you Kendall!

Kendall's Daddy

22

Go confidently in the direction of your dreams.
Live the life you have imagined.

HENRY DAVID THOREAU

Kendall knew what she wanted, even at an early age. Whatever it was, she knew there were two ways to get it. There was the nice way, or the painful way. With the first, you would give her whatever she wanted since she was such a sweet thing. The other way was to be such a pain in the butt that you would ultimately just give in to her and allow her to have whatever she wanted just to get out of the painful situation that she was putting you in. She could use either way to her benefit with the utmost grace.

Kendall had her dreams. Her love of reading led to many of them. She would read about things and want to experience them herself. She was always reading, not only one book, but sometimes two or three books at a time. She shared her dreams with her family frequently. As often as family could, Kendall was given the opportunity to follow these dreams.

Kendall imagined her life in a glorious way. She was always on an adventure. Riding her bike to and from school, she was never simply going in a straight line. Every side street was ridden on. If a bump could be jumped it would be. And anything that looked like it could be a fun place was explored.

Making things fun and exciting was a way of life for her. Nothing was ever ordinary. If it could be done a different way, it would be and her way would be more exciting, never boring, and always more fun. Kendall made sure her family was always involved in her dreams and adventures.

Kendall lived her life exactly like she imagined it would be, how her dreams showed it would be, and how her family allowed it to be.

So be like Kendall. Live your life as you have dreamed it would be, the powerful person that you are.

Kendall's Daddy

23

Family isn't about whose blood you have.
It's about who you care about.

TREY PARKER AND MATT STONE
SOUTH PARK, IKE'S WEE WEE 1998

Ever since my daughter Kendall died, family has become very important in my life. Not only immediate family but also this newer "extended family"; that is, anyone I come in contact with that has been put in the same situation. It seems that whenever I hear about a child dying, I become very sad. It doesn't matter if it is an acquaintance or a perfect stranger's child. Sadness overtakes me.

I am not a strong person and the flood of emotions upon learning of a child's death takes over my body. I am traveling the road of the most horrific situation and when someone else joins me on it, I become sick and heartbroken all over again.

The memories of Kendall's short childhood come back. The happy times, the crazy times; then the sad time when she was with me no more. Now another person is about to go through the same. I wish that they didn't have to do this. It is terrible. The circumstances of a child dying are unfair.

The new family is about to start the long journey of life without their child. I become heartbroken for them. I feel close to them. I have an understanding of what they are about to go through. I care for them. But, there is nothing I can say to them to make them feel better or lessen what they are going through. I just hope that ultimately they can make it through.

Family means a lot of things. It doesn't just mean that you are related, or have the same blood. It means that you have things in common. I feel close to others who are on the same journey as me, the journey of the long lonely road of being a childless parent. I care for them and hope that they will find the way.

The road is going to be a rocky one, with many starless nights and dark corners. Then when things become calm, a star will shine.

Kendall's Daddy

24

*I am called to live in order to know rather
than trying to know in order to live.*

REV. JOHN R. CLAYPOOL

At first you just need to know everything. The what,
where, why and the how. How did it happen? Why
did this have to happen to me? What did I do wrong?
Where are they now?

In the beginning you feel you need to know these
things so you will understand. You feel you need to
understand so that you can go on and live your life.
These feelings compel you to go on with the hope that
at some point you will know the answers, have calm and
will be able to live again.

The hardest thing that I have ever done is giving up
the thoughts of needing to know "the whats, the wheres,
the whys, and the hows." Eventually, you will be able to
live with the anticipation that sometime you will know.
At special unexpected times as you live, the rainbow will
get brighter and you will start to understand. But these
special times cannot be forced, they just arrive.

Giving up these words of question frees your heart
to live life, accept your new life, and attempt to live it
with the joy that you once had in it. You will always want

to know these things, but you are now allowing yourself the freedom to set them aside for the time being. The answers simply can't make a difference.

If you knew the answers could you prevent anything? Why worry about things that you have no control over? You did your best, wanted the best and that's how you lived your life. Your heart is saddened because of the change. Accepting the change is not easy, but so necessary.

The calm never comes when you try so hard to *know* in order to live. The calm comes when you live with the understanding that someday you *will know*. It's the anticipation of knowing that will bring calm to your heart.

Kendall's Daddy

25

*They whom we love and lose
are no longer where they were before.
They are now...Wherever we are.*

ST. JOHN CHRYSOSTOM

When your child dies ahead of you, wishing that they were here will always be a major part of daily life. This single event in your life alters your love forever. You'll find yourself wondering when and if you will ever see them again; then, only seeing them in your dreams for a brief period of joy, and not wanting to wake up, so you may enjoy it forever.

You have lost the feeling that your child will be forever with you. The joy-filled dreams of the future times that you will have together as you both travel the road of life, frolicking in the wind, or playing on the beach building your dream castle together are gone. They will never be by your side again.

Remembering the decisions that needed to be made after Kendall died, how to go on with life, how to regain control. *Control of what,* I'm still not sure of. Basically, just what to do next? All these decisions, though simple, were most difficult. But the answers would somehow come. I'm not sure how, but the answers were always the correct ones for the time and with these answers life seemed to align. I truly believe that Kendall had a major part of this.

Our children have the answers because they are the answer.

Wherever they are, in your home, the college dorm, in their own home with the family that they have started, your children may be out of sight at these times, but they are still with you. Like this, your child is ahead of you on your journey and they still will be with you wherever you are. They may be on your shoulder, your hip, or over your heart, but they will always let you know they are with you in the simplest, silliest, loving ways. Never far away, just become silent and they will make noise.

Kendall's Daddy

26

Our children change us...
whether they live or not.

LOIS MCMASTER BUJOLD

"Oh God, what do I do now?" That was my first thought after Kendall was born. All the schooling and books can't prepare you for this event. It is a life-changing occurrence that you savor for the rest of your life. This is when your education really begins. The what-ifs run through your mind and you start to prepare for everything.

Even from her rough start, Kendall started teaching me things about me, life, family, and the world that I thought I already had a pretty good grasp on. Boy was I wrong. Looking back, I didn't know anything or at least that is the way I felt. Then slowly, she started to guide me, showing me the way. The way to being a person that is responsible, sharing, and patient.

It is a wonder how strong a bond that is developed between a parent and child. You think that a parent is the one that guides a child into adulthood, but think about it. From the day your child is born, it is actually they that guide you into adulthood. Then you travel the world together allowing them the freedom to live life, to experience life, and to enjoy life to its fullest extent possible.

Then the unthinkable happens, your child dies. What is the first thing that you think of? You're right, *"Oh God, what do I do now?"* You have to start life all over again. This time, without any guidance from them; yet somehow, the guidance still comes. Kendall is still here guiding me along the pathway of life. As usual with her, the path isn't straight, but who cares?

She is always on my mind. Her death, just like her birth was a life-changing occurrence. My life took another drastic turn and is now somewhat lonelier. She now is teaching me still to enjoy life, not to take it so seriously, and it is okay to be silly. You really don't know when, where, why, or how your trip together is going to end. So why not enjoy it as best you can? It is good to be a child even as you grow older. So it is a full circle. With their birth they transform you into an adult and then with their death you become like a child.

Kendall's Daddy

27

When you become quiet it just dawns on you.

THOMAS EDISON

One of the joys of being a Daddy is being able to take the time away from your life and spend it in your child's life. You develop the bond of parent and child that lasts for eternity. One of my joys was riding a bicycle with Kendall in a seat behind me. In the beginning of the ride we would chat about our day and what we did. Then Kendall would get quiet. I would ask her if she was still there behind me. Her quietness would overtake me and the world around us would open up. The flowers and trees would appear, the clouds would form wonderful shapes, and you could hear and see the birds. In her quietness she found that nature just dawns and abounds in all its beauty.

Just being together is a wonderful thing too. No words are needed. Your sense of speech takes a break and the other senses start to work. They show you so much. You just have to watch and wonderful things appear. These things were there before, but in the clutter they were hidden. Quietness is an awesome thing. Things just seem to appear out of it.

Out of the quiet, dreams appear. Daydreams. What a

wonderful way to spend time. Thinking of the places you would love to be. On top of that cloud floating by or in an inner tube floating down a peaceful river.

In your quiet you are able to think and talk with yourself without the distractions of the infinite things that bombard you in your everyday life. You learn from yourself, you're able to see the solution as things dawn on you.

Just as Kendall was a chatterbox, she also had her quiet times. She figured out just as the quietness of the dawn opens a new day, the quietness of the mind opens a new world.

Kendall's Daddy

28

Love does not begin and end the way we seem to think it does. Love is a battle, love is a war; love is a growing up.

JAMES BALDWIN

Kendall, I miss growing up with you.
Kendall's Daddy

29

And laying his hands on him he said,
"Brother Saul, the Lord Jesus, who appeared
to you on the road by which you came,
has sent me so that you may regain your
sight and be filled with the Holy Spirit."

ACTS 9:17B

Kendall was a very loving person. She would always be doing or making something for you, or just wanting to be close to you. Often during these close times, she made sure she was touching you. One of her favorite things was to wake me up in the morning and whisper in my ear to meet her on the couch in the living room. There she would have our pillows set, a blanket, and the TV on her favorite cartoon station. Then we would cuddle together and be as close as we could possibly be. Every once in a while she would reach back and just pat my leg with her hand, making sure I was there and to comfort me.

The next time I felt the power of the hand being placed on me was the worst day of my life. It was at the Memorial service for Kendall. I felt the need to be a part of the service. I had no idea why, because this was in no way like me. I was not a public person, and would never think about speaking in front of a group of people. Kendall's cousin Adam sent a graceful poem about *moving on* that I was going to read at the service. At the chosen moment I stood up, took a deep breath and walked to the lectern where I was to read the poem. A very powerful person walked with me and as I stood there, attempting to gain the strength to accomplish the unbelievable for me, he placed his hand on my back. As he did this, my heart rate came down, my breathing became normal, and calm came to me. With Pastor Durwood's hand on my back, I read the poem completely and was told that my voice never quivered and was very powerful.

Every holiday, birthday, and even just regular days, memories flood back of the days I had with Kendall. February 27, 2005 would have been Kendall's 18th birthday. A person's 18th birthday is a special one, as it's when they become an adult. I wasn't looking forward to that day. Late the night before I decided that I really needed a hand to help me through the next day. I honestly didn't expect the help that I would be receiving.

It was, as usual in the time of need, with Durwood again. I felt his hand on my shoulder as he told me he loved me. With his gentle touch and calming words I was comforted. He backed away, to give me space, I thought; but the next moment I found myself in the midst of a very powerful group of people placing their hands on either me, or the person standing between them and me, forming a chain of hands that led to me. Again, my heart rate came down, my breathing calmed, and I felt the presence of peace.

The power of touch, be it by hand, hug, or presence is an awesome thing that brings your sight back to you in many different ways.

Kendall's Daddy

30

Some memories are realities, and are better than anything that can ever happen to one again.

WILLA CATHER

Is there ever a day that goes by that you don't remember something from the past? It may be a good memory, bad memory, or just something that spurs you on. Something may happen that triggers a memory. That can either make your day or completely ruin it.

The weekend after Kendall's memorial service we took a boat ride with friends. I really didn't want to go. I didn't know what I really wanted to do. I'm not sure if I do now either. It was in the summer time, so there were rain showers around. It was a quiet ride, until we saw two rainbows side by side: a large one and a smaller one next to it.

Out of the mouths of children come outstanding thoughts at times. Kendall's best friend's brother, Brian, saw it first and said, "Look! God is teaching Kendall how to make rainbows!" To this day I haven't found two rainbows together. At that moment, that sight was something needed and is now a lasting memory.

Every time I see a rainbow, I think of Kendall right away. The rainbow sign was started by Kendall prior to her death; she would draw them on everything and everywhere. When she got a new box of crayons it would be the first thing she would draw with them. So now, the rainbow is a very strong and lasting memory of Kendall.

There are signs that can bring on the flood of memories of loved ones. They range from colors to objects to places. A cloud may float by, the wind may ruffle a feather, or you may drive by someplace that was your loved one's favorite place to be. All these bring on the memories that are much needed to keep your special person's love inside your heart alive. Certainly memories can make you sad and you may start to cry, but in the end you can smile as you remember special times and places. Memories allow things of the past to always be in the present.

The reality of memories is that they keep with you those special things that you never want to lose, but have. I just wish some of my memories were realities.

Kendall's Daddy

31

Here is the test to find whether your mission on Earth is finished: if you're alive, it isn't.

RICHARD BACH

I have started to wonder when my mission on earth will be over; often wishing it would be soon. But I wake up every morning, so it still isn't finished. I want to be someplace else with someone else, but I keep waking up on Earth. I'm not sure if it would be good or not to know when your mission will be over.

While they are still here, children whose mission seems to be cut short have an air about them. They are special people with knowledge of life that exceeds that of other children and often adults. Kendall, I am told, had an understanding about religion and life that was outstanding. She had a trust and knowledge that her life would be taken care of after her mission was finished. I never thought her life would end when it did. I'm not sure if she knew when her mission would end, but she lived life to its fullest right up to the end, and I'm sure she is living the same way in Heaven.

Are there signs that your life on Earth is about to end? The months before Kendall passed away, as a family we did many special things, creating many memories.

Family pictures taken, vacations enjoyed, and as I look back, good-byes were said. On one of the trips we took, we went to my sister's home for Kendall's cousin Sam's high school graduation. When we were leaving for the drive home, Kendall gave my sister a hug that seemed to go on for eternity. A simple good-bye or was it a sign?

These old souls teach so much to everyone around them while on Earth. Possibly their mission while on earth is to help those in need and when they have done this, their mission starts to come to an end. I know Kendall taught me a lot while we were together. As I continue to go through life without her, I believe she is still teaching me and guiding me.

Is something around the next corner to make your mission continue? You will never know. Who decides when your mission will be over? Not you. If you're reading this, you're alive and your mission here on Earth isn't finished. So, as well as I can, I am continuing on my mission and striving to live life as Kendall taught me to and would want me to.

Kendall's Daddy

32

Death is more universal than life;
everyone dies but not everyone lives.

A. SACHS

Did you live life? What was your life like? Do you look forward to life or death?

Kendall made me live life! I think she knew about death. We were always playing, be it from dolls to basketball. Going on adventures either real ones or make believe ones was always fun. Kendall had an outstanding imagination that made these adventures an awesome experience.

Experiencing life was a priority with Kendall; she made sure that the experience was shared by all. If you weren't doing anything, she included you in her activity. Or after the fact would tell you all about it with no detail left out.

Always wanting to be with family, she lived life with them and through them. From being on the football field or on the sidelines, she lived through her cousins. On the way to and from school I had the privilege of riding bikes with her. She even made these times an adventure. She knew every side-street, bump, tree, and sign on the way to and from school. Often she would make a boring ride home the funniest ride of your life. She wanted you to laugh and enjoy your time together. There wasn't a sign hung from a pole that wasn't hit with her helmeted head.

One major thing that I have learned from Kendall is that since you know you are going to die, make the most of your time on Earth. Live life to its fullest. Have fun. It is the way they would want you to be. This is a simple wish, but it is much easier said than done.

Living life to its fullest is a challenge after losing your loved one. Especially when it was they who helped you do this while they were with you. But why not be like them and be spontaneous? Don't care what others think. Does it really matter? Who decides what is normal? Who cares what other people think if they don't like what you are doing? If they say something to you, just tell them "Whatever!"

Kendall's Daddy

33

Not all that wander are lost.

J. R. R. TOLKEIN

After Kendall's death I developed the need to wander. I worked in Miami, a two hour drive from home. Along the route is a small gallery of a gentleman who takes only black and white photographs. His name is Clyde Butcher. I stopped in the gallery one day and saw the most awesome photograph. It is called "Moonrise over the Everglades." It is a black and white photograph of the moon over the Everglades taken during the daytime, something that Kendall and I had discussed many times. "Why can you see the moon during the day?"

Many things happened that day. The first was that I had found this piece of art, that now hangs in my house, which can cause me to remember and contemplate. I also found out that Mr. Butcher started taking only black and white photographs after his son died. "Moonrise over the Everglades" was the first photograph that he took after joining the club. Lastly, in front of the gallery is the most beautiful spot to sit and meditate. In the middle of the Everglades was the most peaceful and quiet spot. When able, I always wander to this spot to give me time to think, remember, and talk to Kendall.

The year Kendall would have been 18 I missed the signs. After her birthday, I couldn't figure out what was wrong with me. Finally, I decided I needed to go on a road trip—to wander. I decided to do some things with my truck which would require me to see two people near the town where Kendall was born and lived her first two years of life. It was a three and a half hour drive, so I had plenty of time to think. I got done with my first stop and it was lunchtime. Since I was in the town that we lived when I bought Kendall her first Happy Meal at McDonald's, I decided to celebrate Kendall's 18th birthday like I had her 1st birthday. *I* ate the Cheeseburger Happy Meal this time.

After finishing what I wanted to do in the area, I started the drive home. On the drive home, I had more time to think. The day was a good one I decided. I had gotten two things done for the truck, something I think that Kendall is behind. It is "our" toy that we are able to have fun together with. But I figured out that the real purpose for my wander that day was to have that Happy Meal with Kendall. The truck was just an excuse for me to get to that McDonald's.

Sometimes you just have to wander to find yourself.

Kendall's Daddy

34

You can complain because roses have thorns,
or you can rejoice because thorns have roses.

ZIGGY

I am told that childbirth is quite painful. This is the first sign that roses do have thorns. The mother must endure the thorns of pregnancy to receive the rose of life. Throughout this time she deals with many thorns: morning sickness, backaches, and the big one—labor. But the rose is well worth the battle.

While growing up, Kendall had many thorns. Some she was given and didn't deserve. Others she grew while traveling through her short life. Kendall's medical problems were a thorn in her side, but she never let them slow her down. She saw the rose in them all.

Every child grows and gives their parents thorns at times. These times are just learning about life and attempting new things. In the parent's eyes these thorns may hurt, but a child must learn, and to learn you must make mistakes. Be glad that your child grows thorns, so that they may learn and you may guide them in the garden of life. Finally, when they are in full bloom, you let them go and watch them travel out of your garden.

It is hard to see the rose many times because the

thorns may be bigger than the rose. When Kendall died, the thorn was much bigger than the rose. At that time, it was hard to see *anything* that could be good about this horrible thing. It didn't happen quickly, but down the road I have seen some roses. She changed my life and I learned many things during our time together. I remember her daily, the thorns that we endured together and the roses that we had. I think of the thorns that will appear in my everyday life, but I know Kendall will help me see the roses.

Just as I guided Kendall in her life and someday would have had to let her go, she too guided me and has let me go. But Kendall is still watching over me and showing me that thorns do have roses.

Kendall's Daddy

35

*Outings are so much more fun when we
can savor them through the children's eyes.*

LAWANA BLACKWELL

Kendall went on a school bus for a field trip with her class from Tommie Barfield Elementary School. On the trip home, the bus driver chose a bumpy road to avoid traffic. Well, as you can imagine the bus was really bouncy and the adult chaperones didn't like the ride. There was a big "to-do" with the school about the driver not being safe. I listened to the chaperone's stories and how they went on about all the children being scared and getting sick. Then I sat down with Kendall and talked with her about her feelings about the ride. Kendall said she wasn't scared, and thought it was fun bouncing down the road. Through the eyes of a child, things are so much more fun.

Kendall's summers were full of outings. At least once during the summer, she would be with my sister and her three children. Kacie, the youngest, had a horse. Being the adventurous one, Kendall wanted to ride a horse too. Arrangements were made and Kendall and Kacie went to the stable and each had a horse to ride. Kendall did an outstanding job of controlling the horse and directing it to do the correct thing. But, after a while, enough was enough, and her eyes said she was finished. I'm not sure if she was scared of this beast that outweighed her 100 times, or she had enough and wanted to go on her next outing.

Being with Kendall on most of her adventures and observing them myself, our eyes never saw the same thing. Even the routine trip to the store was completely out of this world when she described the route we took, the places we passed, and the fun we had taking it. You knew she was having fun on every adventure; she had the biggest smile on her face.

This child's eyes were not afraid of anything. They had no fear; always looking for the highest tree to climb to have the best lookout to watch for pirates or swimming underwater for as long as they can, to make it into the underwater cave at the far end of the pool.

Never be afraid of what others think of you on your outings. If it might be fun—DO IT!

Don't do what others expect of you. It is okay to color outside the lines, or go the length of the mall doing cartwheels. Life shouldn't be boring. If it is, perhaps you should take a child someplace and get *new eyes*.

Kendall's Daddy

36

If you can give your son or daughter
only one gift, let it be enthusiasm.

BRUCE BARTON

Kendall was not limited to any activity that she wanted to do. This, despite the hand she was dealt in life. Her every endeavor was with her whole heart, mind, and body. She knew how to enjoy life and the world. Her enthusiasm was in overflow mode all the time.

If Kendall got excited over an activity, gift, or really anything, the biggest smile would overtake her face and she would just shiver from enthusiasm. I don't know where this came from, but it happened deep inside her body and erupted out the top.

A passion for life, and enthusiasm. Kendall had it. Sometimes I think she wanted to do it all because she was worried there wouldn't be enough time to get it all in. Maybe she knew something. We always seemed to be planning something or going somewhere. The night before a trip was going to be a sleepless night with a lot of talking about the much anticipated activity.

A nighttime ritual was to listen to a music tape to fall asleep. Quite often, this wouldn't be enough, and she needed time to chat. Well, with all of her excitement, she would usually outlast the other person. Finally, she would have to be told it was time to turn her brain off so it could get some rest. She just couldn't wait for the next day to come.

Even the night before a regular school day, Kendall often would have trouble falling asleep in anticipation of the next school day. Being one that really didn't like or appreciate school, I thought this was unbelievable. She surely didn't get this trait from me, but it was great. Reading was a passion with her, always having one and often two books going at the same time. She hated to be sick and miss school. If Kendall were to miss school, she was the one who asked for her homework to be picked up, so she could do it. Her enthusiasm for education carried outside the schoolhouse also. She always wanted to learn.

Even in her playtime, Kendall gave it her all. She was always out of breath and sweating. Physical activity, no matter how demanding, was challenged with the enthusiasm of all her other quiet activities.

Let them shine. Allow children to be enthusiastic. Don't hold them back. Kendall was always allowed to be who she wanted to be; holding back was not in her mindset. I'm not sure if I could have held her back. She charged forward, often too fast for me to keep up.

Kendall's Daddy

37

*Angels can fly because they
take themselves so lightly.*

G. K. CHESTERSON

I wonder if they know how special they are. Most of the time the saying "perfect little angel" fit to a 'T,' but oh boy, there sure were some times that made you wonder. Kendall was not serious all of the time. She would joke around with you. Like the time at the dinner table with my parents right after my father got his hearing aid.

Kendall understood what the hearing aid was for; so during dinner she started a conversation with my father and then in the middle of a sentence started to only mouth the words. My father thought his brand new hearing aid broke already but it was just Kendall keeping life light.

Kendall understood a lot for such a little girl. She would always have a presence in the room, but she would never be obnoxious or need to be the center of attention. She would be quiet in the background, watching and listening. I think she had figured out that you could learn so much by just doing this. Even if it was outside playing a game, she would watch before she would join. Once she figured out what was going on, she'd join in and be great at it.

Angels don't boast about what they can do. They don't want the attention. Quietly they carry out their job, and the gratitude they receive comes from the thought that they did a good deed. They seem to prefer to always give of themselves and never want anything in return. Kendall always was giving special little gifts to whomever she came into contact with. She enjoyed doing things for others and floated high when she received a smile in return.

Everyone has angels watching over them. Look up at the blue sky with wisps of angel wings floating by, listen to the trees rustle and watch them sway in the summer breeze. Even on a rainy day they are flying high above the rainbows. Angels don't consider what they do as a heavy burden, but rather as a light endeavor that allows them to make their loved ones and friends happy.

So why not be like an angel, take life lightly. It helps you to get through the days and weeks of loneliness just a little easier. Plus when you take life and yourself lighter you can fly like an angel and be closer to them.

Kendall's Daddy

38

Be who you are and say what you feel,
because those who matter don't mind,
and those that mind don't matter.

DR. SEUSS

It is okay not to be your old self; you have a new self anyway. Your world is upside down and changing rapidly. The people in your life that matter to you will understand and accept the new you. You're trying to figure out who you are and the new vocabulary that was placed on you. Sometimes saying what you feel will help you figure out who you are.

Usually, the ones that don't matter don't know how to ask or talk to you; they don't know what to say or how to act, so all they offer you is silence and distance. They may be able to ask about your life and await your answer. However, if their jaw drops and they take off running upon your reply, then this will be your sign that *they don't matter.*

A brave and caring person will ask, then stay for the answer. But, very often they really don't know how to ask. *So, how do you ask?* That is a very good question. For me, please don't start out with "I know how you feel ..."

Everyone is different. You *don't* know how I feel. *I* don't even know how I feel. Some others that have lost children don't like the generic, "How are you?" Start with a caring statement or question. "Is life getting easier?" "How do you make it through the day?" Or just say how life sure sucks sometimes.

When you find someone who cares enough to ask, feel free to be whoever you are on that day. Tell it like it is; people who matter won't mind and will understand. Be honest with them. If you haven't figured out how you are, tell them, "Beats me, but when and if I ever figure it out I will tell you." Lonely, hurt, in pain, lost, and confused are all words that may guide you and help your friends learn how you are doing.

With your new life of being a childless parent, you will likely develop new friends. The old ones who stay by your side are the caring and understanding ones. Those who matter won't care what you say as long as you say what you feel. The new friendships that develop come from those who are already on the road that you are just beginning and won't care what you say to them because they already understand your new world.

In your new world you are like a child with much learning to do. Feel free to say how you are feeling. You have a lot of figuring out to do and it will help. Just as a child doesn't know who they really are until many journeys and miles down the roadway of life, you need this time and distance.

When you find someone who doesn't mind, hold onto them. Remember those that matter are special people and likely have an angel on their shoulder too.

Kendall's Daddy

39

*If you can't sleep, then get up and
do something instead of lying there
and worrying. It's the worry that
gets you, not the loss of sleep.*

DALE CARNEGIE

Sleepless nights. You awake for no reason with nothing on your mind. You either weren't dreaming or you can't remember what you were dreaming about, but as soon as you wake up your child is on your mind. You can't get back to sleep and you just lie in bed worrying. The world is upside down and it doesn't look like it is going to straighten up anytime soon.

My sleepless nights began June 21, 1996 and haven't stopped yet. Some nights I am able to sleep through the night, but others I wake up and lie in bed worrying. When that happens I might wander the house, watch TV, or perhaps write. The last seems to be the most beneficial for me. Being a daddy, I continue to worry about Kendall to this day.

Even at Kendall's Memorial Service I worried about her. After the service we went into the hall for the reception and I was standing with my niece, Kacie, and they had started to bring the food out. There were many young children there and someone had made PB & J sandwiches for them. I thought this was great, and knowing that Kendall got to be quite a handful when she was hungry, I started to ask Kacie to make sure that Kendall got one of those sandwiches. Luckily, I caught myself before saying that to Kacie. I'm not sure who would have been more upset, Kacie or I.

You will never stop worrying about your child. I hope that I never do. Something that helps is that I talk to Kendall when I first lie down in bed. Just thanking her for being with me throughout the day and guiding me through life's trials. I have trouble with prayer, so I just talk. It helps free the mind of the worries that you gathered throughout the day and releases them to someone that can help.

Kendall always had a special prayer that she developed to help get her to sleep. It went like this: *"Dear God, Please let no bad things happen to my family or friends. Please help me to go to sleep fast. Please let my (music) tape be very, very fast. Amen."* She let her worries go about her family and friends. This allowed her to get to sleep and stay asleep throughout the night. The negotiator in Kendall made the deal that if she wasn't asleep by the end of the music cassette she would listen to, she could come fall asleep in bed with Nan and me. Luckily, we have a big bed.

So if you can't sleep find an activity that takes your mind off worrying until the sun comes up.

Kendall's Daddy

40

Challenges are what make life interesting;
overcoming them is what
makes life meaningful.

JOSHUA J. MARINE

The death of your child is a challenge that no one
hopes ever to deal with; in fact they never fathom
that it might even happen. Suddenly, your world is
thrown into chaos. You're trying to figure out what life
is all about, what your purpose in life is now, and what it
is going to be.

Living life without your child is an all-new world;
more difficult than the one before. Everything looks different, everyone acts different and you wish you weren't
in the new world. *I want my old world back!* You find yourself searching and seeking, but often never finding. Life
is a challenge now, but not one that is more interesting.

I enjoyed my life much more before Kendall died. I
know it was much more interesting with her traveling
the road of life with me. Nothing was ever the same with
Kendall. Kendall had many medical challenges that she
faced. All but the last one did make life more meaning-

ful. I learned how precious life is, and to appreciate every breath even more.

I will be forever indebted to the doctors who kept Kendall traveling down the road of life. I marvel at them overcoming the challenges that faced them. They conquered them and gave me a bright young star who made my life meaningful. These doctors were truly gifted men.

Second to the death of your child, I think the act of just plain parenting is next in line for the challenges of life. From their birth all the way to adulthood, you're going to have challenges. First, figuring out what a parent *is*. And then *how* to guide your child through life. Their behavior, the mighty tantrums they will throw and the grief they are going to put you through, is going to challenge your body and soul. But once you make it through the challenges, you find out that with them life is truly meaningful.

Never give up the opportunity to face challenges with your child; they are the ones that make life meaningful.

Kendall's Daddy

41

Mama always said life was like a
box a chocolates,
You never know what you're gonna get.

FORREST GUMP

Unlike many couples, Nan and I decided not to find out the sex of our new baby during the pregnancy. We wanted to be surprised, or maybe it really didn't matter. When Kendall was born, we were just happy that she was finally here. Everything worked out in the end during her birth. I definitely wouldn't have tasted her like a chocolate, and put her back for anything. She lit up my world.

Being our first child, and in the end our only child, I really didn't know what to expect. I never imagined that she would be like she was or how much she would change my life. She definitely would have had the right to bite the chocolate of life and put it back. Kendall sure was given some bad chocolates.

However, being the chocoholic that she was, Kendall chewed them up and never spit them out. Being such a positive person, Kendall accepted whatever was thrown at her, dealt with it, and moved on. She knew what she wanted out of life and took nothing less.

On one of our trips to my sister's home, Kendall and her Uncle Rich were sitting at the kitchen counter about to have some cookies and milk. For both of them, their favorite cookies were Oreos. So Rich got everything set and had Kendall sit next to him at the counter. He went through the bag of cookies and placed on Kendall's plate all the broken pieces. She let him finish and then looked at him and just said, "I don't think so!"

She knew the pieces couldn't be dunked in the milk, which was the best part. Rich *learned* about Kendall that night and Kendall got her "whole cookies" to dunk in the milk. Rich hadn't known what was inside that little box of chocolates next to him; he soon discovered a strong-willed but kindhearted little lady.

Even being the strong-willed little girl that she was, Kendall could, however, be bribed with chocolate. I will admit to being a lazy parent and not wanting to fight with her to eat breakfast before going to school. Just to get her to eat something, she would be allowed to have some cookies or a chocolate shake. I'm not sure which she loved more, life or chocolate. You never had to ask her what type of ice cream or type of dessert she wanted. As long as it had one or more types of chocolate in it, it would be fine.

Just as Kendall didn't mind what was inside the chocolates, it didn't matter what was inside the book of life to her. She liked it all. Life does give you some strange fillings once in awhile; as soon as you taste it you may not like it. But in the end it will be good. The bad taste that is often left initially, will, after time, become a sweet memory that you will savor for eternity. Even the bad memories will become tasty treats of the mind.

I will never put a chocolate back in the box; I want every precious memory they provide.

Kendall's Daddy

42

The soul would have no rainbow
had the eyes not tears.

JOHN VANCE CHENEY

I remember the first time I saw your eyes; it was in a very cold environment of the delivery room. Even in that environment when our eyes met, yours showed love. You were the most awesome thing that I had ever had anything to do with. You gave me purpose.

Kendall. Because of the curves she was thrown in life she had to have several eye operations so that she would be able to see properly. The operations left her eyes bloodshot and teary, but in the end gave her the sight that she deserved. During every recovery period of the operation, Kendall would love to draw and a rainbow was the first thing to be drawn on each piece of artwork.

The hardest decision I have ever made in my life was the decision to leave for work the night before Kendall passed away. To this day I can't say that it was the right decision, but it was made, and I regret that decision to this day. The very last time I saw Kendall's eyes was that night, June 20, 1996. I can still remember sitting on the couch in the living room with Kendall, holding her, attempting to comfort her, and wanting things to be so different. I left for work only to receive the worst tele-phone call of my life the next morning.

Traveling home, dreading to go to the hospital made it an unbearably long journey. Arriving at the hospital I went into a room and found Kendall lying on a bed. I couldn't help her anymore. All I wanted her to do was open her eyes and give me one of her big hugs. I had to see her eyes one more time. I cuddled with her one last time and did the scariest thing in my life. I lifted her eyelids to see her loving eyes. The tears started flowing down my cheeks. These tears started to build Kendall's rainbows in my soul.

Life allows you to suppress grief and memories until you are able to handle them. Needing a change in my life in an attempt to find it again, I changed jobs. Because of the new job, I had to go through some training. In this training we had to have instruction on the handling of hazardous material. In particular, this day the subject of instruction was how to handle human remains and body organs that needed to be transported. BAMM, in an instant I was right back to that hospital room with Kendall. I really was not able to handle the subject very well that day, and it took me quite awhile to process this situation.

The tears that I shed when Kendall was with me and the tears that I shed after she went to Heaven have allowed my soul to develop. Kendall must have known what rainbows are all about. Now she is up in Heaven, and when tears from Heaven fall, rainbows appear, and my soul is recharged. On a sorrowful day even if there is no chance of rain, I will take the garden hose, spray it into the air, and make my own rainbows.

I need rainbows. I guess that my life will continue with tears in it, but with grace they will be happy tears. You see, you need to experience life in many ways, often tearful ways, to have the rainbows in your soul become energized.

Kendall's Daddy

43

People are like stained-glass windows. They sparkle and shine when the sun is out, but when the darkness sets in their true beauty is revealed only if there is a light from within.

ELISABETH KUBLER-ROSS

You meet people at odd times and in stressful situations throughout your life. On the dark day that Kendall passed away, the ambulance and fire department were at the house doing all that they could to keep Kendall here on Earth. One of the people that fought for Kendall was Don Jones, one of the most loving and caring men that I have ever met. After the tragedy quieted that night he has continued to care for our family.

Keeping Kendall's memory alive became of prime importance not only for me, but everyone who she had touched. The mothers of children who attended Kendall's elementary school wanted to do something at the school for her. As it happened, Don not only tried to keep Kendall here on Earth, but is also the one who keeps her alive at the school. He is an artist and creates the most beautiful stained-glass pieces of art.

The piece that he designed for the school is a sailboat sailing under a rainbow, traveling toward beautiful mountains. It hangs in front of the office of the librarian of the school, where it can be seen by all who enter the library. This is the perfect place for it to be. Kendall was an avid reader and at least once a day she would be in the library.

Since we needed something beautiful at our home for us to see Kendall's beauty, we commissioned Don again to do a stained glass piece for our front door. Like the library piece, this one also has a sailboat, but overhead if you look very closely you can see a cloud in the shape of an angel protecting it and all aboard from harm.

Both of these stained glass windows are hung in places that offer their beauty both when the sun is out, and also during the dark of night. During the day, the lights of the library are on allowing all to see. When the school is closed and the lights are out, the librarian's office light shines through it, keeping its beauty showing to the out-side world. Our front door is always visible during the day with the window's beauty showing. As the sun is setting and the last sunlight is passing through it, the facets in the window cast beautiful rainbows throughout our house. Then as night falls and we turn lights on inside, its beauty continues to shine even greater to the world.

Tragedy brings darkness to your life, but in time, beauty will be revealed to you and from you.

These pieces of stained glass art as well as Don Jones are some of the most precious things in my life. They truly allow me to see that the most special beauty is revealed when darkness sets in. Kendall's memory is alive. Her beauty shines on, even in the darkness.

Kendall's Daddy

44

*The best and fastest way to learn a sport
is to watch and imitate a champion.*

JEAN CLAUDE KILLY

Kendall spent a lot of time with her older cousins. Not enough time if you asked her. Much of her time with them was focused around sports. Kendall was proud of her cousins and watched them with such intensity in an effort to fully understand what was going on. In a short amount of time she picked up whatever sport they were participating in.

At home she wanted to be involved in everything. It started at the playground. She would quietly find a piece of equipment that took no skills and use that while watching other children on the swings, slides, and monkey bars. In a short amount of time, she was off the easy stuff and challenging the playground. This was the start of her figuring out that if she watched someone who already could do something, she could pick up on how to do it quicker. Pretty soon, she was the champion of the playground and all the other children were watching and learning from her on how to be a monkey and be across the monkey bars in short order.

Kendall wasn't afraid to try anything, but to start she

first watched and then conquered. We went to gymnastic, tennis and swimming lessons. We practiced and played on soccer, basketball, and baseball teams. When the boys next door started a street hockey game, she got her skates on and practiced skating on the sidewalk and watching them. After a bit of being a spectator, she decided she could do it. After yelling at the boys to get them to stop, she asked if she could play. The bigger kids always protected Kendall and these boys did the same. They got her fully protected with gloves, pads, and helmet. I'm not sure how she even skated with all the protection she had on. Off she went, out into the street and was skating with the experienced players and doing a heck of a job.

For such a young individual, Kendall had figured out the secret to life. *Don't pretend to know everything right off the bat. Sit back, take it all in, and then jump in and conquer.* She had figured out that life is just one big game. The easiest way to become a champion is to learn from and be like that person.

Others watched Kendall as she went through life. They saw how she conquered any situation that was thrown at her, and now often use that mindset in their life today. I remember the countless hours on the monkey bars that Kendall spent. It was hard in the beginning but after awhile it was easy for her. She just needed time to put together the skills she learned from watching others with the strength and confidence that she had. Kendall was a very strong-willed and focused young lady. Nothing would stop her once she made her mind up.

I learned these things from Kendall and take them with me each morning as I attempt to conquer the world just as she did. As I stay in the game of life, I look back at what I have learned from the champions in my life.

Kendall's Daddy

45

*If I could be anything for one day
I would be my dog, Blaze.*

KENDALL JEANNE MOLL

"Daddy, let's get a puppy!" A parent's nightmare; you know down the road who will end up taking care of it. I knew this and didn't care. I wanted one too. Off we went to many pet shops and dog shows. Kendall wanted a Dalmatian. Her favorite movie at the time was *101 Dalmatians*. After talking and listening to many Dalmatian owners, we were convinced that it really wasn't the type of dog for us, and with a little persuading

Kendall was convinced likewise. She was such a family person that she liked the idea of getting a Boxer, like I had when I was growing up. Now that we knew the type of dog, we had to find one. It was an easy find. At one of the many dog shows that we went to, we found out that there was a puppy available near our home.

Off we went; Kendall fell in love with the puppy and they became best of buddies. But there was a problem coming up with the right name, one that really fit. So one day while watching a TV show there was a person named Blaze. The name of Blaze stuck because the puppy could run as fast as blazed lightening, and had a diamond-shape blazing on her nose. So, our life with a dog began.

As with any puppy, many things had to be taught. I got the tedious stuff; potty training, walking on a leash, and obedience training. Kendall got the fun stuff; playing with toys, fetching, and the hardest of all—how to use the doggie door to go outside. This took some time to accomplish. Kendall tried and tried to call and coax Blaze from the other side of the door, but to no avail. Finally, Kendall decided to demonstrate the proper use of a doggie door to Blaze. Down on all fours Kendall went and proceeded to walk towards the door, bang the door open with her head, and then she jumped through the open door, just as she wanted Blaze to do.

This took a couple of demonstrations from Kendall and then finally Blaze followed her out the door the same way. I'm not sure who gained the most benefit from this accomplishment, Blaze for being able to go outside or

Kendall for learning patience and understanding on how to get a difficult task accomplished. Both sides won.

Kendall cared for Blaze as much as Blaze took care of Kendall. Many a thunderstorm Kendall would be found under a piece of furniture with Blaze, attempting to calm her from the storm. Blaze was Kendall's protector too. If someone was rough with Kendall, or Blaze thought they were going to hurt Kendall, she would step in and with her teeth showing, gnarl at them and make them stop.

Blaze has since passed away, and we now have Angel. The name fits most of the time. Kendall wanted to be her dog for a day and in many ways Angel has Kendall in her. She always wants to cuddle, kiss your face, and her favorite spot to sleep is right between Nan and me. I think Kendall got her wish, but it is more than for just one day.

Kendall's Daddy

46

I believe in God, only I spell it Nature.

FRANK LLOYD WRIGHT

The tomboy in Kendall kept her outside for much of her free time. She loved wide-open spaces. Close to our house was a stand of pine trees where she and her friends in the neighborhood built a fort and had rope swings between the trees. Kendall was often up a tree or swinging between them. It seemed she felt free here and loved to be in nature with all its splendor. When Kendall was old enough she joined the Girl Scouts and of course wanted to go on the camping trips. Well, they were luxurious camping trips; they slept in cabins, not tents, and had bathrooms. Kendall loved nature, but I'm not sure she would have ever gone on another camping trip if she had to go to the bathroom in the wide-open nature.

Our adventures together were always outdoors. We went on many fishing trips with Kendall and she would always be in the thick of things. She was such a curious person who wanted to learn all about everything. When the fish was caught she wanted to touch it, but always caring for it and wanting it to go back in the water to live longer.

Any new experience was game to Kendall. When we planned a trip to my sister's in Maryland in the winter, Kendall read many books that described the snow and how pretty it was. She wanted to play in it, feel it, and taste it to experience its beauty.

Kendall's understanding of God and nature is likely one of the only places where we had some distance between our thoughts on it. Kendall was comfortable inside church as well as outside in His nature. She could feel close in both places. For me, I am much closer when I am outside in the world's natural beauty. I feel much closer to God with the coolness of the ground, rather than a pew on my back.

A goal of mine is to someday have a cabin in the mountains, so I can be closer to nature. Yes, it will have electricity and running water. I don't want to get back to nature that closely. I just want to enjoy nature and all its beauty. Plus, I feel if I am on top of a mountain, I will be closer to Heaven and to Kendall. But, I know that Kendall is everywhere. Wherever I am, she is. So when I am watching the fish jump behind the house or the snow-fall, I know she is there with me.

Being one with nature was something that Kendall understood. When it was warm and the swimming pool looked inviting, Kendall would be the first one in. She really liked this natural thing; she must have, because she would be in the pool all the time, just like she came into the world, naked as a jaybird. Au natural! I guess this was just another way for Kendall to get back to nature.

Kendall's Daddy

47

One should either be a work of art,
or wear a work of art.

OSCAR WILDE

Kendall was a piece of art; I really think she was a piece of work. You never knew what she was up to; she was game for anything and loved to surprise. She always had an art project going too, usually with my mother. They enjoyed their time together doing the arts and craft thing. Not only did we get refrigerator art from school, but also from home. Each and every piece was always displayed. These pieces are still displayed all over our house.

Kendall loved to make presents for everyone, not only to hang on the wall but to wear at times too. I still wear a t-shirt that was a project of hers. Now understand, Kendall was born in the 1980s and really wasn't too involved in the 1960s culture where my tie-dyed t-shirt would have come from. But, one day on television she saw one and thought it was cool, so she and my mother got one of my white t-shirts and got a kit to tie-dye it.

My birthday is in October and Kendall passed away in June. That very year Kendall gave me clothes. On one of the shopping trips that she and her mom took, she saw a shirt that she knew would look good on me. They bought the shirt and it was put away for my birthday. That birthday, although very sad, was made brighter because of the thoughtful person that Kendall was.

Maybe Kendall knew that I would never be a work of art, so she made sure that I would always be wearing a piece of art. I continue to keep Kendall's thoughts of either being a piece of art or a piece of work alive. I too now, am into the art of surprise and keeping people on their toes.

Although, not visible, I wear pieces of permanent art. I have two tattoos, and they reflect my thoughts of Kendall. As my love for Kendall will never fade, my two tattoos will always shine. On my right shoulder blade is my guardian angel, with flowing skirt and Kendall's initials hidden in it, and halo above her golden hair. Then over my heart is her heart; of course it is purple, with angel wings surrounding it. The tattoo over my heart was tattooed on Kendall's 18th birthday. I chose to do it on that date, because I knew that is exactly what she would have been doing on that date, with or without approval.

The angel wings were done with flamed edges to show that Kendall had a little devil in her. After all, she would have been getting tattooed knowing that her mom would have been having a fit and her Daddy thinking it was cool. Kendall is still prompting me to wear pieces of art, even if others can't see them. I guess this is another one of the things that Kendall has brought out in me, the art of surprise and being game for anything that comes up. Or just maybe, she is trying to make me a piece of art.

A piece of art is something that is beautiful to look at, something to appreciate, and something that will make you think. With those things in mind, I know Kendall was a piece of art and I wear her love with pride.

Kendall's Daddy

48

*To us, family means putting your arms
around each other and being there.*

BARBARA BUSH

The power of hugs is an awesome thing. It helps you just feel better and allows you to let go. When you are feeling weak and someone puts his or her arms around you, you regain strength and are able to continue on. It is a sign of caring. You don't have to say anything, just do it.

More than the ability to *say* anything, the ability to just *be there* for someone is more beneficial. Sometimes you just need bodies around you to hold you up. One of my favorite quotes is "I will never let school stand in the way of my child's education." Kendall learned a lot about life and family from taking trips to be with her aunts, uncles, and cousins. Kendall and her cousins may have been cousins by birth, but are siblings by love. Whenever there was a special event in someone's life, the family would gather. Championship sporting events, high school graduations, and really whatever Kendall could convince us that she needed to go to.

Kendall was proud of her family and loved to be with them. She also loved her quiet time by herself to read and draw rainbows. She had her functions that the family would come to also, such as graduations, Girl Scout ceremonies, and many school events. Kendall loved getting the congratulatory hugs from doing well just as much as she loved to give them out.

Kendall was, and still is, the guardian angel always there watching over, making sure you were okay. She was always available to put her arms around you and be there. For such a young person, Kendall truly knew the meaning of family.

I haven't felt the warm hugs from Kendall in quite a while, but her warmth is still around. At holidays, family meals, and special occasions there is always a candle burning brightly. It is our reminder of the light and warmth that Kendall brought into the family. Like Kendall in the mornings, sometimes the candle is a little difficult to get started, but watch out, once it is lit it is off and running.

As a balloon sent above with love, so does the warm air from the candle reach high to Heaven and Kendall. These symbols from her family represent our arms going around her and being there with her.

Although I never had the opportunity to embarrass Kendall by hugging her in front of her friends at a later age, while she was with us she didn't mind if you hugged her in front of them. In fact, if you were absentminded enough to forget to hug her good-bye, she would remind you and make sure she got a hug before you left. Even those times that I went to eat lunch with her at school and watch her play on the playground, we would hug good-bye just before she'd go back into the classroom. Kendall always wanted to make sure that you knew she would be there for you with her arms wide open.

Kendall's Daddy

49

Aerodynamically, the bumblebee shouldn't be able to fly, but the bumblebee doesn't know it so it goes on flying anyway.

MARY KAY ASH

Kendall didn't know. She didn't know that she wasn't supposed to play contact sports. Who was going to stop her anyway? While playing soccer and in the midst of the pack of little players would be Kendall trying her hardest to get the ball. I never wanted to miss a moment of the game, but it was hard to watch when the ball was in the air and she would be lining up to head the ball. The thoughts of a trip to the hospital flew through my mind. When her cousin Adam started to play football you could see the wheels turning as she began to figure out how she could play, and her mom and I trying to figure out how to deal with this.

The rough and tumble world of wrestling was Kendall's adventure land. She loved to wrestle, rolling around on the ground to see how dirty and messy she could get. Kendall didn't know that she was a girl sometimes, and I'm glad. When she wanted, she could out distance any girl as to who was the coolest tomboy. She

116

stood her ground with boys and was not afraid to go head to head with all the boys on the team. They all respected and accepted her as just one of them.

But, she could be a real lady when she wanted, *well needed,* to be. She loved to play with dolls, have tea parties, and be the prim and proper young lady that the world thought she should be.

She always made up her own mind about everything. It didn't matter what others or even the world thought. If she thought differently, that's the way it was. When we bought our first house and were deciding what colors to paint the rooms, Kendall decided that her room was going to be purple. We were told that purple wasn't a good color to paint a child's room. It leads to poor behavior. Well, her room got painted purple. Kendall liked the color and flew with it, disproving the behavior issue with the color purple.

Despite all Kendall's medical issues, she didn't know the world to be any different, so she decided to take on the world and was well on her way to conquering it. The setbacks that were encountered along the way, although major at times, Kendall treated as only minor. They never stopped her quest for knowledge; her mind was always in the search for more information. She always had such a positive outlook on everything; you would never know what really had happened in her short life.

Her body went through much hardship, besides the normal everyday child aches and pains, the operations to correct her birth defect and subsequent revision to it, and finally her eye operations. All these were accepted by her as she flew right past.

At such a young age she wasn't suppose to have figured life out. She wasn't suppose to fly with the bumblebees, but no one told her that, so she did and has flown away.

Kendall's Daddy

50

A true friend is someone who thinks that you are a good egg even though he knows that you are slightly cracked.

BERNARD MELTZER

Mackle Park is the gathering place on Marco Island for moms to bring their children to burn off some of the endless energy that they have. It seemed that Kendall needed to take a trip to the park at least once a day, so she could run and play. This allowed her mom and me to take a break from the entertaining of a young child. She would be at ease running, jumping, and climbing over everything by herself there. One day there was a new girl at the playground. Kendall never had a problem talking or playing with someone new.

The new girl was Sara; she had just moved to the Island. Kendall and Sara soon became the best of friends and never separated again. Kendall loved to entertain and Sara was a great accomplice. Sara understood Kendall and Kendall likewise with Sara. It always seemed that Kendall would be her normal goofy self, and Sara would be laughing.

You would have thought the two of them would be twins for they were never far from each other. But, Sara's red hair and freckles were a far cry from Kendall's blonde hair and fair skin. As time went on, the play at the park soon turned to taking bike rides together, having sleepovers, and birthday parties always planned with each other in mind.

Kendall's grandparents had a great pool and deck area for Kendall and Sara to play. In the summertime you would always find both the girls sitting beside the pool at a small table eating their lunch and giggling. The giggling often was the result of Kendall attempting to convince Sara to go skinny-dipping in the pool after lunch. Sara would let out a big, "NO WAY!" and they both would start giggling loudly. These are moments Sara most likely figured out that at times Kendall was just slightly cracked.

Even with Kendall's death, I think Sara and Kendall are still true friends. They both are still very close at heart, both to each other and to me, for the smiles that they produced. We are still involved in Sara's life, keeping up with dreams, goals, and accomplishments. We have become family.

Many times families have weird occurrences. Shortly after Kendall passed away, Sara told us that she had called her grandmother to talk about losing Kendall. Since losing Kendall, Sara and her grandmother have an even greater bond now. It seems that when in the third grade, her grandmother had lost her very best friend too. Besides the family bond, they now have a bond of understanding.

Sara's high school friends understand how deeply Sara loved and appreciated Kendall as a friend. For her 18th birthday they all gave money so that Sara would have a memorial brick at the Christmas Box Angel Statue in the cemetery here on Marco Island. They know how deeply the feelings Sara has for her slightly cracked friend Kendall go.

Kendall's Daddy

51

It is all very well to be able to write
books, but can you waggle your ears?

JAMES MATTHEW BARRIE

There wasn't a day that went by that Kendall didn't have a book or two on hand reading them simultaneously and amazingly keeping the stories separate. Kendall was an excellent reader, reading well above her age level. Reading was something that she enjoyed, both pleasure stories and educational books. Her mind was always thirsting for knowledge.

At her school each year they would have an Authors and Artists Night. Local artists and authors would come, talk with the children, and guide them in the mastery of each realm. A project for that night was a book that she wrote by herself. It was titled *The Confusing Seasons*. The story was about Sara, her best friend, and Sara's fictional little sister Kim when the weather pattern was completely confused. It turned out that Mother Nature was sick and the two girls found her and nursed her back to wellness and the weather corrected itself.

In Kendall's room, it's still in her book collection. The author by whom many of the books she enjoyed were written is Beverly Cleary. Kendall dedicated *The*

Confusing Seasons to Beverly Cleary. Kendall's book was very well written and illustrated, but she couldn't waggle her ears.

The only person Kendall knew that could waggle his ears was her grandfather. Although he wasn't an author he could entertain her for hours waggling his ears in the midst of one of their many conversations about life, sports, or just about any subject. He would do it and then Kendall would get a stern look on her face, concentrate very hard, attempt to waggle her ears, and then give up after asking, again, "How do you do that?"

Kendall's love of reading was turning into a fascination for writing too. She always had a pad and pencil with her and would be writing notes and little stories. At the Authors and Artists Night, she would be intently engrossed in everything the author would be saying and upon arrival at home would tell anyone that would listen what he had said. Her stories were very good, all surrounding her family and life. But she still couldn't waggle her ears.

Kendall strove to be the best she could be and get good grades in school. Mrs. Keegan, her third grade teacher, could see that in her too. She would always come home with refrigerator art and stories with A's and smiley faces on them. The teacher comments on the stories were "great job," "I like your transitions," "the support and examples for your reasons are good," "well organized," and "keep up the good work." Kendall was as proud of these comments as I was for her in receiving them.

Perhaps, this joy of writing is another of the many things that Kendall has planted the seed of into my mind. I write to free the entrapped thoughts of my mind. Writing gives me time to think and reflect, and remember that Kendall couldn't waggle her ears.

I'm not sure if I am able to write books very well, but I do know that I can't waggle my ears either.

Kendall's Daddy

52

Twinkle, twinkle, little star,
How I wonder what you are.
Up above the world so high,
Like a diamond in the sky.

JANE TAYLOR

Well, now I know the words to the song. I could never get the words out right when Kendall would make me sing it to her, as she would be trying to fall asleep.

She would get so upset with me when I would sing the wrong words or the right words in the wrong order. I would always say to her, let's just listen to the song on the cassette tape, but I never got away with that.

Her bedtime ritual was just that, a ritual. It was cast in stone and couldn't be broken, or her getting to sleep would be a challenge. Of course, my singing the song terribly didn't help matters either. Puff was always there, right next to her face, the smelly thing that it was. That was another thing that disturbed the ritual, when Puff had been washed during the day. He usually had that certain smell that made all things seem okay.

Prayers were next, and then the singing of "Twinkle, Twinkle Little Star" just before the last big hug for the day, and hopefully we were off to sleep. Many a night there would also be a conversation about the world, life, family, and just about anything else she could think of to avoid falling asleep.

These conversations brought back the memories of when Kendall first joined us in the world. At the time we didn't have this ritual, so after trying numerous ways of lulling Kendall to sleep, I found the easiest was just having her lie on my chest and she would drift right off to sleep. Being new to this daddy-stuff at the time, we were still having these talks while she was falling asleep. Only, it was just me talking to her about the world, life, and family. What a great time we were going to have, and what the future held for us.

Kendall's eyes were always twinkling. One of Kendall's conditions caused her to have a lazy eye. To correct this we would have to place a patch over her good eye to make the weak one stronger. As you can imagine, she really didn't enjoy having these patches on. To make it less traumatic, I would decorate the patches with different figures or scenes on them so they were prettier than just a plain old band-aid. During the holidays there would be a Christmas tree or pumpkin on it, whatever fit the day. Once she even had a Teenage Mutant Ninja Turtle covering her eye.

The patches worked and later Kendall's eyes were perfect. Her eyes opened the world to me and now they are opening the heavens to me. On cloudless nights I lay in the front yard looking up into the heavens and watching the twinkling stars. Then, as I am in bed still attempting to remember the words to the song, I talk to Kendall and say goodnight to her. The nightly ritual still goes on and will continue on into eternity.

My little star, up above the world so high, Kendall you are my diamond in the sky.

Kendall's Daddy

53

*I may not have gone where I intended
to go, but I think I have ended
up where I intended to be.*

DOUGLAS ADAMS

I think that once I figure out where I intend to go, my life might end up there. In the midst of my fourth career, I am still not sure if it is where I should be. All my careers have in one way or another helped people with life. From protecting them, helping them enjoy it, taking them to distant places, and now helping them provide their families a place to live. I am traveling to an intended place, but I don't know where or what it is.

Kendall helped and is still guiding me along the way to that place I'm supposed to be. She, like all children, help put life into perspective if you just listen to them. Along the way, they might make you take detours, but maybe you were supposed to be there anyway.

The pathway of life is never straight. Detours, road-blocks, and bumps in the road are always going to be there. The purpose of this no one ever knows. The curves all serve a purpose and someday you may know what the purpose was. Life is like one of Kendall's bike rides; often sidetracked, down every street, around every tree, and under every sign. Finally she made it to where she planned to be. But, I think she did intend to go to all these places along the way. She loved life, wanted to enjoy it, and wanted to experience everything. When she was ready or when it was the right time, she finally made it home.

I am finding my life going in different directions; it is scary. I am along for a ride that I'm not sure I'm in control of. Maybe one of these new directions is where I'm intended to be. Will somebody please tell me?

I didn't intend to be where I am. But who would want to be where I am? Am I going to end up where I intended to be? Life has many mysteries.

Being a parent, you are never going to go where you intend in a very straight line. The road of life for both you and your children will lead in many different directions. There will be an end to it and all the different routes will all have a meaning someday. You may not have wanted or deserved the route you were given, but it will make you stronger when you get to your intended place.

Perhaps if you could take on life like a child and have no place to be and don't care when you'd get there, life would be more enjoyable. Everyone makes it to their destination sometime, so kick back, relax and enjoy the ride.

As I sit here writing, I am thinking that maybe this is the detour I'm suppose to be on at this moment. And this detour has showed me that Kendall didn't intend to be where she is, but she whole-heartedly deserves to be there!

Kendall's Daddy

54

You won't realize the distance you've walked until you take a look around and realize how far you've been.

ANONYMOUS

I remember the day my unexpected journey started. My first thoughts were, "I don't want to take this journey, let's end it right now." Somehow, from somewhere, I remained on the road, traveling this long, lonesome, crooked road without Kendall.

In my early stages, I just tried to make it through the day, so I could get to bed and put an end to the day. As I fell asleep I would always wish for a visit from Kendall. I'm not sure why they came when they did, but on select nights Kendall would visit me in my dreams. These visits kept me walking down the road hoping for another one in the near future. As time passed, my goals lengthened; I purposed to making it through a couple of days and then into weeks.

The pathway I'm taking has yet to become easy, but it is becoming slightly more tolerable. Everyday life, memories, and dreams today seem to be stuck in the time warp of the era when Kendall last held my hand as we went for a walk. She will always be a nine-year-old bundle of energy, full of life, and often untamable. I didn't want her any different then and I don't want my memories any different now.

It has been many years since I began this journey of being a childless daddy. I am still attending the events that Kendall would have been at. I see her friends and classmates going through life and attaining their goals. All this leads me to wonder: the many wonders of being a daddy, the hopes, the dreams, and the sleepless nights. How would I have coped with it all?

Many holidays, birthdays, and family events have passed. The road has been a long one, but time is passing by quickly. Time has put a lot of distance in between the present and the past. As the distance gets greater, I continually think that I am one day closer to being with Kendall again. I don't know when or where that day will be, but it is getting closer.

As I sit and reflect on my life, both before and after Kendall passed away, it truly has been a long journey. Her first birthday, the first steps she took, and her first word all mile markers in our life together. Now as the road is getting longer, her 18th birthday and her high school graduation have passed. Even greater mile markers lie ahead.

The distance is getting greater and will continue to grow. I look back and remember the past. It truly has been a long time since Kendall and I were together, but somehow I have made it further down the road than I have ever thought possible. The road is still as crooked and full of potholes, but with distance the travel has changed. Now I think about the past and wonder about the future, knowing that I am putting distance on the past and making the road to the future shorter.

Kendall's Daddy

55

Father and Daughter

Listen and teach. Protect and let go.
Believe and admire. Love and know.
A father's approval is a daughter's greatest treasure.
A daughter's security is a father's deepest desire.
Know that you are loved

RAPHAELLA VAISSEAU

Listen. . . . Remember those first sounds after her first breath? Oh what a cry it was. That first time she let the world know it was time to watch out for a new life has appeared to be reckoned with.

Teach. . . . the ways of the world. Be a strong, powerful person and know where that power comes from. Not to be afraid to ask for what she wants and let her feelings be known. It is okay to ask for something not on the regular menu at McDonald's.

Protect. . . . her from the falls that she might take. Not wanting her to get hurt or be hurt. Feeling the pain as she went through the trials, tribulations and surgeries that she accepted as life's follies.

Let go. . . . As painful as it is, it has to be done. Never saying Good-bye; Good-journey maybe, but likely just *Later.* You listened to her, taught her, protected her and now she is on her own road. She will travel farther away than she has ever been before. But yet is never far away.

You believe in her. She knows what is right and wrong, how to make the best decision for any situation that will arise, and who to ask for help. Admire her. She is part of you. Be proud.

She always wants to do her best for you, to make you proud, and for you to approve of what she has done. With the past she has shown you what she will do in the future. So get ready. When she came home from school and showed you that she read a chapter book, got all A's on her report card, or tried something new that even you haven't done yet, these accomplishments weren't the treasure she was after. The treasure was that big hug of approval and trip to the ice cream store with you. *That* is what it was all about.

To be safe and secure is the deepest desire any daddy ever has for his daughter. For her never to be sick, or to have a tear in her eye or pain in her heart is all that you desire. These are hard things to accomplish, and you do your best to succeed. You are not alone in your most important job of life: the raising of a daughter. Both you and she have a Guardian Angel to help and guide along the way.

However hard it is, know that she loves you.

Kendall's Daddy

56

I've learned that good-byes will always hurt,
pictures will never replace having been there,
memories good and bad will bring tears,
and words can never replace feelings.

ANONYMOUS

I'm sure I would have had to do this at one time in our
life and I wouldn't have wanted to do it then either. I
am told that I need to do this, so that I may continue on
in life with less pain in my heart. So this is a long time
coming, nine years and 168 days, and I still don't want
to do it. But I can't avoid the hardest thing in my life
anymore.

I remember the first time I saw you. Mommy had to
have a C-section, so we were in the operating room for
her to have the procedure. I don't remember the sight of
you coming out of her belly and being whisked by me
to another room to be put in a bassinet under a light. I
think at the time I was just trying not to faint, so I don't
really remember that moment very much. But, when they
came and got me to come see you, I saw the most precious gift that I had ever received. I said, "Hi" to you and
we became bonded for eternity.

Kendall, I am so sorry I wasn't with you when you died. I hope you weren't scared when it happened. There is nobody that can really tell me what the experience is completely like. Many have experienced the process, but the ones that have written about it have never completed the journey themselves.

I think about you every day, often crying. But as time goes by, I find myself just staring out into space and thinking of you, smiling, and wondering. Wondering what you would be like, what I would be like with you still in my life and knowing that life would be just a little happier with you still here.

I still worry about you. Are you happy? What is Heaven like for you and what do you do every day there? I am finally coming to the realization that I can stop worrying. You are better off than I am. I know that happiness is what every daddy wants for his little girl; I just wish I could have provided it for you. Even though I am saying "Good-bye," you will always be the one that makes my heart beat.

You made my life complete. I did my best with the decisions I made in regards to you. There is no training on how to be a daddy. I regret some of the decisions I made now, but I didn't know the outcome at the time. I sure would have made different ones if I had known.

I am wandering in my life right now and need to find the pathway to a happy life. I know this is what you would want for me and will help any way that you can. The opening line in "The Road Less Traveled" by M. Scott

Peck, MD is "Life is Difficult" Boy, he sure hit the nail on the head. The road is never smooth; I just wish the potholes weren't so big.

Since we're saying Good-bye, some changes need to be made. You would have turned 18 years old, graduated high school, left for college, and started your own life. Just like if you were here and this had all really happened, your bedroom is going to be the new guestroom/office in our house. It will still have your presence in it. Don't worry; you will always be welcome home with open arms.

I knew this was going to be a hard thing to do and probably hurt a little too. But, I think you, as well as I, need to say Good-bye so we both can grow and do what is destined for us. I know you will still be around in memories and pictures and yes, I'm still going to cry every once in awhile.

These words are comforting, but they are only a small part of us, and will never take the place of the bond that we have.

Kendall, I need you to do one thing for when we are finally together. I'm not sure when that will be, but you know me, and I need to plan things out. If you could, please find out if the Milky Way is dark or sweet chocolate.

Kendall, I Love and Miss You! Good-bye for now.

Kendall's Daddy

The Author

 Roger was born in Tucson, Arizona while his father was stationed at Davis-Monthan AFB. His childhood was primarily started in Ft. Lauderdale, FL and finished up in Chatham, NJ.

He has a BA in Criminal Justice from Seton Hall University which he received while working as a police officer in his home town of Chatham, New Jersey. After getting married, the decision was made to return to sunny south Florida. A career change led him to become a cabinet maker in the marine industry. Wanting more out of life, he went back to his childhood dream. Following family footsteps, Roger returned to flying.

After the death of his only child, Kendall, he wanted to stay close to home. Currently, he is working on Marco Island, Florida, and enjoying being able to go home for lunch and play with Angel, the family boxer.

Roger's e-mail address is rainbowhtr@aol.com.